The Teacher's Quotation Book

little lessons on learning

collected by
Wanda Lincoln
& Murray Suid

*As long as you live, keep
learning how to live.*
                    Seneca

DALE SEYMOUR PUBLICATIONS

One's friends are that part of the human race
with which one can be human.
George Santayana

෫ To Jan—a sister and a friend

Copyright © 1986 by Dale Seymour Publications.
All rights reserved. Printed in the United States of
America. Published simultaneously in Canada.

Order number DS03603
ISBN 0-86651-316-7

DALE
SEYMOUR
PUBLICATIONS
P.O. BOX 10888
PALO ALTO, CA 94303

9 10 11 12 13 14 15 16-MA-95 94 93

contents

introduction

According to one bit of wisdom:

Good things, when short, are twice as good.
Baltasar Gracián

So we'll be brief. This book aims to give teachers, librarians, and administrators a ready source of entertaining yet practical quotations about education.

If, like us, you enjoy reading wise sayings for their own sake, consider this advice:

The only way to read a book of aphorisms without being bored is to open it at random and, having found something that interests you, close the book and meditate.
Charles Ligne

There are countless possibilities for putting this freeze-dried wisdom to work:

• **Create a positive climate for learning and teaching.** Try posting maxims in classrooms, hallways, the office, the cafeteria, bathrooms, and on bulletin boards throughout the school. Here's one for the library:

The next best thing to knowing something is knowing where to find it.
Dr. Johnson

- **Set the stage for learning activities throughout the curriculum.** For example, you might begin a science unit on observation with this chalked on the board:

> Is ditch water dull? Naturalists with microscopes have told me that it teems with quiet fun.
> *G. K. Chesterton*

Or let this be the keynote for a session of oral reports:

> Be sincere; be brief; be seated.
> *Franklin D. Roosevelt*

- **Spice up home-school newsletters with funny, serious, or provocative fillers:**

> I find television very educating. Every time somebody turns on the set, I go into the other room and read a book.
> *Groucho Marx*

> Educate your children to self-control...and you have done much to abolish misery from their future lives and crimes from society.
> *Daniel Webster*

> The chief object of education is not to learn things but to unlearn things.
> *G. K. Chesterton*

- **Address behavior problems with the wisdom of the ages.** Take tardiness:

> He who is late may gnaw the bones.
> *Yugoslav proverb*

Or gossiping:

> To speak ill of others is a dishonest way of praising ourselves.
> *Will and Ariel Durant*

- **Dress up report cards with inspirational messages:**

> Human nature is ever capable of improvement and never able of being made perfect.
> *John Clare*

- **Greet students each morning with an upbeat thought-of-the-day.** You might present it orally or write it on the board:

> Why not go out on a limb? Isn't that where the fruit is?
> *Frank Scully*

- **Evoke class discussion or essays with a mind-stretching quotation.** You might ask students to explain why they agree or disagree with this opinion:

> Fame is proof that people are gullible.
> *Ralph Waldo Emerson*

- **Add thought-provoking messages to make a point on a handout.** For example, you might caption a reading list this way:

> To read without reflecting is like eating without digesting.
> *Edmund Burke*

- **Motivate action at a faculty or PTA meeting:**

> Nothing will ever be attempted, if all possible objections must be first overcome.
> *Dr. Johnson*

- **Cheer up a colleague whose favorite lesson just fizzled:**

> Success is getting up just one more time than you fall down.
> *Anonymous*

- **Leave a bit of advice for your substitute:**

> The savage in man is never quite eradicated.
> *Henry David Thoreau*

Warning: Be skeptical as you flip through this volume. Recall the sage advice of the great aphorist Marquis de Vauvenargues:

> Few maxims are true in every respect.

Even this one.

an invitation

Quotations are like shells on the beach. No matter how many have been collected, there are always more wonderful examples left to find.

If you would like to share your favorites, please send them to us. Perhaps we can include them in the next edition.

We don't know, of course, that there will be another edition. But we're inspired by that great twentieth century philosopher (and baseball player) Yogi Berra, who said:

The game isn't over until it's over.

the quotations

ability ⚮

There is something that is much more scarce, something rarer than ability. It is the ability to recognize ability.
Robert Half

Do what you can, with what you have, where you are.
Theodore Roosevelt

Native ability without education is like a tree without fruit.
Aristippus

The king is the man who can.
Thomas Carlyle

You cannot teach a crab to walk straight.
Aristophanes

absence ⚮

A short absence is safest.
Ovid

Absence makes the heart grow fonder.
Thomas Haynes Bayly

1

Out of sight, out of mind.
Anonymous

Achilles absent was Achilles still.
Homer

achievement ⚙

Having once decided to achieve a certain task, achieve it at all costs of tedium and distaste. The gain in self-confidence of having accomplished a tiresome labor is immense.
Arnold Bennett

It is not impossibilities which fill us with the deepest despair, but possibilities which we have failed to realize.
Robert Mallet

My mother drew a distinction between achievement and success. She said that "achievement is the knowledge that you have studied and worked hard and done the best that is in you. Success is being praised by others, and that's nice, too, but not as important or satisfying. Always aim for achievement and forget about success."
Helen Hayes

The more you do, the more you are.
Angie Papadakis

The way to get things done is not to mind who gets the credit of doing them.
Benjamin Jowett

Our mistakes and failures are always the first to strike us, and outweigh in our imagination what we have accomplished and attained.
Goethe

He conquers who endures.

Persius

The world recognizes nothing short of performance, because performance is what it needs, and promises are of no use to it.
Philip Hamerton

action 🕸

Nothing will ever be attempted, if all possible objections must be first overcome.
Dr. Johnson

Be content to act, and leave the talking to others.
Baltasar Gracián

Doubt, of whatever kind, can be ended by action alone.
Thomas Carlyle

Malice will always find bad motives for good actions. Shall we therefore never do good?
Thomas Jefferson

The great end of life is not knowledge but action.
Thomas Huxley

The finest eloquence is that which gets things done.
David Lloyd George

The shortest answer is doing.
Proverb

Those who are quite satisfied sit still and do nothing; those who are not quite satisfied are the sole benefactors of the world.
Walter Landor

admiration 🕸

We admire the other fellow more after we have tried to do his job.
La Rochefoucauld

We always like those who admire us, but we do not always like those whom we admire.

La Rochefoucauld

advice 🐝

In giving advice, seek to help, not please, your friend.

Solon

Advice when most needed is least heeded.

Anonymous

If you can tell the difference between good advice and bad advice, you don't need advice.

Laurence Peter

In America, the young are always ready to give to those who are older the benefits of their inexperience.

Oscar Wilde

It is not good to give one's advice unasked.

Janet Stuart

Listen to all, plucking a feather from every passing goose, but follow no one absolutely.

Chinese proverb

Never take the advice of someone who has not had your kind of trouble.

Sydney Harris

People who ask our advice almost never take it. Yet we should never refuse to give it, upon request, for it often helps us to see our own way more clearly.

Brendan Francis

Tact is the ability to make advice agreeable.

Anonymous

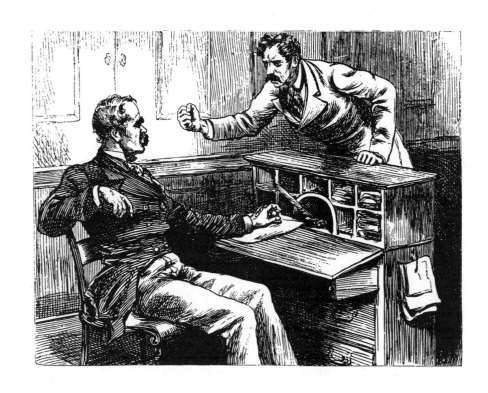

Keep cool; anger is not an argument.

Daniel Webster

anger 🕸

People who fly into a rage always make a bad landing.
Will Rogers

When anger rises, think of the consequences.
Confucius

answers 🕸

It is a good answer that knows when to stop.
Italian proverb

No answer is also an answer.
German proverb

appearance 🕸

Cleanliness and order are not matters of instinct; they are matters of education, and like most great things, such as mathematics and classics, you must cultivate a taste for them.
Benjamin Disraeli

We are charmed by neatness of person; let not thy hair be out of order.
Ovid

art 🕸

Art flourishes where there is a sense of adventure.
Alfred North Whitehead

Every child is an artist. The problem is how to remain an artist once he grows up.
Pablo Picasso

A man paints with his brains and not with his hands.
Michelangelo

Anyone who keeps the ability to see beauty never grows old.
Franz Kafka

Art is a higher type of knowledge than experience.
Aristotle

Art is an idea. It is not enough to draw, paint, and sculpt. An artist should be able to think.
Gurdon Woods

Art is meant to disturb.
Georges Braque

Art is not a thing; it is a way.
Elbert Hubbard

Art is the difference between seeing and just identifying.
Jean Norman

Great artists are people who find the way to be themselves in their art.
Margot Fonteyn

I shut my eyes in order to see.
Paul Gauguin

Never lose an opportunity of seeing anything that is beautiful.
Ralph Waldo Emerson

The great artist is the simplifier.
Henri Amiel

The most accomplished monkey cannot draw a monkey, this too only man can do; just as it is also only man who regards his ability to do this as a distinct merit.
Georg Lichtenberg

There is no *must* in art because art is free.
Vasily Kandinsky

We cannot create observers by saying "observe," but by giving them the power and the means for this observation, and these means are procured through education of the senses.

Maria Montessori

attitude ❧

Whether you think you can or think you can't, you're right.

Henry Ford

Acceptance of what has happened is the first step to overcoming the consequences of any misfortune.

William James

No life is so hard that you can't make it easier by the way you take it.

Ellen Glasgow

Put a grain of boldness into everything you do.

Baltasar Gracián

Show me a thoroughly satisfied man—and I will show you a failure.

Thomas A. Edison

The best way to cheer yourself up is to try to cheer somebody else up.

Mark Twain

The fault-finder will find faults even in Paradise. Love your life.

Henry David Thoreau

We can learn something new any time we believe we can.

Virginia Satir

Whatever you blame, that you have done yourself.

Georg Groddeck

When fate hands us a lemon, let's try to make a lemonade.

Dale Carnegie

audio-visual instruction ✍

Image is the great instrument of instruction.
John Dewey

One picture is worth a thousand words.
Anonymous

I hear and I forget.
I see and I remember.
I do and I understand.
Chinese proverb

Even the best of educational TV is limited to offering quantitative improvements in the kinds of learning that existed before it.
Seymour Pappert

books ✍

The book to read is not the one which thinks for you, but the one which makes you think.
James McCosh

A book is like a garden carried in the pocket.
Chinese proverb

Be as careful of the books you read, as of the company you keep, for your habits and characters will be as much influenced by the former as by the latter.
Paxton Hood

Except a living man, there is nothing more wonderful than a book.
Charles Kingsley

Have you not noticed, after many heartaches and disillusionments, that in recommending a book to a friend the less said the better? The moment you praise a book too highly you awaken resistance in your listener.
Henry Miller

11

*To acquire the habit of reading
is to construct for yourself
a refuge from almost all the
miseries of life.*

W. Somerset Maugham

He who destroys a good book kills reason itself.
John Milton

Master books, but do not let them master you. Read
to live, not live to read.
Edward Bulwer-Lytton

Never read a book through merely because you
have begun it.
John Witherspoon

What's a book? Everything or nothing. The eye that
sees it is all.
Ralph Waldo Emerson

Wherever they burn books they will also, in the
end, burn human beings.
Heinrich Heine

boredom ❧

Being bored is an insult to oneself.
Jules Renard

Boredom is the bitter fruit of too much routine or
none at all.
Brendan Francis

Nobody is bored when he is trying to make something that is beautiful, or to discover something that
is true.
William Inge

bragging ❧

Be wiser than other people if you can; but do not tell
them so.
Lord Chesterfield

None so empty, as those who are full of themselves.
Benjamin Whichcote

Talk like Robin Hood when you can shoot with his bow.
Proverb

Tell me what you brag about and I'll tell you what you lack.
Spanish proverb

bullies ৯৪

Those who are fear'd are hated.
Benjamin Franklin

All our foes are mortal.
Paul Valery

The man who strikes first admits that his ideas have given out.
Chinese proverb

careers ৯৪

Every calling is great when greatly pursued.
Oliver Wendell Holmes, Jr.

Whenever it is in any way possible, every boy and girl should choose as his life work some occupation which he should like to do anyhow, even if he did not need the money.
William Phelps

change ৯৪

Most of us are willing to change, not because we see the light, but because we feel the heat.
Anonymous

One must never lose time in vainly regretting the past nor in complaining about the changes which cause us discomfort, for change is the very essence of life.

Anatole France

The only completely consistent people are the dead.

Aldous Huxley

character development &

What you want to be eventually, that you must be every day; and by and by the quality of your deeds will get down into your soul.

Frank Crane

Do not wait for extraordinary circumstances to do good; try to use ordinary situations.

Jean Paul Richter

If rascals knew the advantages of virtue, they would become honest.

Benjamin Franklin

People become house builders through building houses, harp players through playing the harp. We grow to be just by doing things which are just.

Aristotle

People often say that this or that person has not yet found himself. But the self is not something one finds, it is something one creates.

Thomas Szasz

Sow a thought, reap an act;
Sow an act, reap a habit;
Sow a habit, reap a character;
Sow a character, reap a destiny.

Anonymous

People seldom improve when they have no model to copy but themselves.

Anonymous

How few there are who have courage enough to own their faults, or resolution enough to mend them.
Benjamin Franklin

The measure of a man's real character is what he would do if he knew he never would be found out.
Thomas Macaulay

The only time you realize you have a reputation is when you're not living up to it.
José Iturbi

There is nothing so fatal to character as half-finished tasks.
David Lloyd George

To conquer oneself is a greater task than conquering others.
Buddha

To have become a deeper man is the privilege of those who have suffered.
Oscar Wilde

You desire to know the art of living, my friend? It is contained in one phrase: make use of suffering.
Henri F. Amiel

children 🦡

You know children are growing up when they start asking questions that have answers.
John Plomp

Childhood shows the man as a morning does the day.
John Milton

Children are natural mimics—they act like their parents in spite of every attempt to teach them good manners.
Anonymous

When you are dealing with a child, keep all your wits about you, and sit on the floor.

Austin O'Malley

Children are remarkable for their intelligence and ardor, for their curiosity, their intolerance of shams, the clarity and ruthlessness of their vision.
Aldous Huxley

The best preparation for being a happy and useful man or woman is to live fully as a child.
Plowden Report

The parents exist to teach the child, but also they must learn what the child has to teach them; and the child has a very great deal to teach them.
Arnold Bennett

There are only two lasting bequests we can hope to give our children. One of these is roots; the other, wings.
Hodding Carter

There is no possible method of compelling a child to feel sympathy or affection.
Bertrand Russell

Water finds its level, the swallows fly south in winter, children learn.
Leo Tolstoy

We call a child's mind "small" simply by habit; perhaps it is larger than ours, for it can take in almost anything without effort.
Christopher Morley

citizenship ॐ

All that is necessary for the forces of evil to win in the world is for enough good men to do nothing.
Edmund Burke

One thing I know: the only ones among you who will be really happy are those who will have sought and found how to serve.
Albert Schweitzer

The fate of the country ... does not depend on what kind of paper you drop into the ballot box once a year, but on what kind of man you drop from your chamber into the street every morning.
Henry David Thoreau

The purpose of freedom is to create it for others.
Bernard Malamud

The worst sin towards our fellow creatures is not to hate them, but to be indifferent to them; that's the essence of inhumanity.
George Bernard Shaw

civilization ⚿

Civilization is a race between education and catastrophe.
H. G. Wells

If a nation expects to be ignorant and free, in a state of civilization, it expects what never was and never will be.
Thomas Jefferson

classroom environment ⚿

When children enter kindergarten, they should discover that each class is a working, problem-solving unit and that each student has both individual and group responsibilities.
William Glasser

A house that does not have one worn, comfy chair in it is soulless.
May Sarton

Chaos often breeds life.
Henry Adams

Conversation is the laboratory and workshop of the student.
Ralph Waldo Emerson

I like to see a man proud of the place in which he lives. I like to see a man live so that his places will be proud of him.
Abraham Lincoln

We must learn to be still in the midst of activity and to be vibrantly alive in repose.
Indira Gandhi

Noise is one of the essential parts of civilization.
Anonymous

We need to learn to create an atmosphere of freedom without license, in which people are free to be themselves and in which they have a feeling of identification with others who are free to be their unique selves.
ASCD Yearbook, 1962

classroom management 🔊

Anyone can steer the ship when the sea is calm.
Publilius Syrus

That government is best which governs the least, because its people discipline themselves.
Thomas Jefferson

The first idea that the child must acquire, in order to be actively disciplined, is that of the difference between good and evil; and the task of the educator lies in seeing that the child does not confound good with immobility, and evil with activity . . . our aim is to discipline for activity, for work, for good; not for immobility, not for passivity, not for obedience.
Maria Montessori

20

Have a time and place for everything, and do everything in its time and place, and you will not only
accomplish more, but have far more leisure than
those who are always hurrying, as if vainly attempting to overtake time that had been lost.
Tryon Edwards

college education ⚅

The aim of a college education is to teach you to
know a good man when you see one.
William James

College education is a form of training which does
not hurt you, provided you study and work hard
after graduation.
Anonymous

Education is something you get when your parents
send you to college. But it isn't complete until you
send your own child.
Anonymous

One nice thing about a college education is that it
enables us to worry more intelligently about things
all over the world.
Anonymous

The young man who is able to work his way
through college is a pretty good bet to be able to
work his way through life.
Anonymous

common sense ⚅

Nothing astonishes men so much as common sense
and plain dealing.
Ralph Waldo Emerson

An unusual amount of common sense is sometimes
called wisdom.
Anonymous

21

Intelligence is quickness
in seeing things as they are.

George Santayana

Common sense is genius in its working clothes.
Anonymous

One of the advantages of being young is that you don't let common sense get in the way of doing things everybody else knows are impossible.
Anonymous

competition &

Competition that involves loss of face, humiliation, or continued failure, often creates anxiety and fear of failure.
Robert Martin

Don't be afraid of opposition. Remember, a kite rises against, not with, the wind.
Hamilton Wright Mabie

Enjoy your own life without comparing it with that of another.
Marquis de Condorcet

The most important thing in the Olympic Games is not winning but taking part...The essential thing in life is not conquering but fighting well.
Baron Pierre de Coubertin

complaining &

It is a great imperfection to complain unceasingly of little things.
Saint Francis de Sales

computers &

Men have become tools of their tools.
Henry David Thoreau

The real danger is not that computers will begin to think like men, but that men will begin to think like computers.

Sydney Harris

There is a world of difference between what computers can do and what society will choose to do with them.

Seymour Pappert

confidence ❧

Be confident, for the stars are of the same stuff as you.

Nicholai Velimirovic

The line between self-confidence and conceit is very narrow.

Anonymous

conformity ❧

A man must consider what a rich realm he abdicates when he becomes a conformist.

Ralph Waldo Emerson

We are half ruined by conformity; but we should be wholly ruined without it.

Charles Warner

conscience ❧

Conscience is the inner voice that warns us that someone may be looking.

H. L. Mencken

Conscience warns us before it reproaches us.

Comtesse Diane

Labor to keep alive in your breast that little spark of celestial fire called conscience.

George Washington

conversation ❧

Don't talk unless you can improve the silence.
Vermont proverb

He who does not understand your silence will probably not understand your words.
Elbert Hubbard

I attribute the little I know to my not having been ashamed to ask for information and to my rule of conversing with all descriptions of men on those topics that form their own peculiar professions and pursuits.
John Locke

The essential charm of good talking rests upon sincerity, spontaneity, and the willing revelation of character.
John Hobbes

(Silence is the) one great art of conversation.
William Hazlitt

Many argue. Not many converse.
Louisa May Alcott

cooperation ❧

Three men helping one another will do as much as six men singly.
Spanish proverb

Help thy brother's boat across, and lo! thine own has reached the shore.
Hindu proverb

We didn't all come over on the same ship, but we're all in the same boat.
Bernard Baruch

We should not only use the brains we have, but all that we can borrow.
Woodrow Wilson

courage

Courage is not freedom from fear; it is being afraid and going on.
Anonymous

Behold the turtle. He makes progress only when he sticks his neck out.
James Bryant Conant

Bravery is being the only one who knows you're afraid.
Franklin Jones

Why not go out on a limb? Isn't that where the fruit is?
Frank Scully

One ought never to turn one's back on a threatened danger and try to run away from it. If you do that, you will double the danger. But if you meet it promptly and without flinching, you will reduce the danger by half. Never run away from anything. Never!
Winston Churchill

Have the courage to live. Anyone can die.
Robert Cody

Tell a man he is brave, and you help him to become so.
Thomas Carlyle

It gives one a sense of freedom to know that anyone in this world can really do a deliberately courageous act.
Henrik Ibsen

creativity &

Creative thinking may mean simply the realization that there's no particular virtue in doing things the way they always have been done.

Rudolph Flesch

If you would create something, you must be something.

Goethe

The creative mind plays with the objects it loves.

Carl Jung

criticism &

Do not remove a fly from your friend's forehead with a hatchet.

Chinese proverb

A form letter used for replying to critical letters:

Dear Mrs. Jones:
Thank you for your letter.
I shall try to do better.

Carl Sandburg

Find the grain of truth in criticism—chew it and swallow it.

D. Sutten

He has the right to criticize who has the heart to help.

Abraham Lincoln

Reprove thy friend privately; commend him publicly.

Solon

The rule in carving holds good as to criticism; never cut with a knife what you can cut with a spoon.

Charles Buxton

To avoid criticism, do nothing, say nothing, be nothing.
Elbert Hubbard

We criticize faults less to correct them than to prove we do not possess them.
La Rochefoucauld

You must not pay a person a compliment, and then straightway follow it with a criticism.
Mark Twain

curiosity &

Curiosity is one of the permanent and certain characteristics of a vigorous intellect.
Dr. Johnson

Children are notoriously curious about everything —everything except...the things people want them to know. It then remains for us to refrain from forcing any kind of knowledge upon them, and they will be curious about everything.
Floyd Dell

Curiosity may have killed the cat, but lack of curiosity would have killed thousands.
James Morrow

Curiosity will conquer fear even more than bravery will.
James Stephens

Nothing is interesting if you're not interested.
Helen MacInness

Curiosity has its own reason for existing. One cannot help but be in awe when he contemplates the mysteries of eternity, of life, of the marvelous structure of reality. It is enough if one tries merely to comprehend a little of this mystery every day. Never lose a holy curiosity.
Albert Einstein

The whole art of teaching is only the art of awakening the natural curiosity of young minds for the purpose of satisfying it afterwards.

Anatole France

curriculum ॐ

Bringing the student's world into the classroom is the most relevant act a teacher can perform.
Marc Robert

I was determined to know beans.
Henry David Thoreau

It is not true that the easier subjects should precede the harder. On the contrary, some of the hardest must come first, because nature so dictates, and because they are essential to life.
Alfred North Whitehead

One ought, every day at least, to hear a little song, read a good poem, see a fine picture, and, if it were possible, to speak a few reasonable words.
Goethe

The pupil who is never required to do what he cannot do, never does what he can do.
John Stuart Mill

The trouble with facts is that there are so many of them.
Samuel Crothers

There are no facts, only interpretations.
Friedrich Nietzsche

We must not only give what we *have*; we must also give what we *are*.
Cardinal Joseph Mercier

What is honored in a country will be cultivated there.
Plato

decision making ॐ

Destiny is not a matter of chance, it is a matter of choice.
William Jennings Bryan

Don't be afraid to take a big step when one is indicated. You can't cross a chasm in two small jumps.
David Lloyd George

I leave this rule for others when I'm dead,
Be always sure you're right—then go ahead.
Davy Crockett

If we are ever in doubt about what to do, it is a good rule to ask ourselves what we shall wish on the morrow that we had done.
John Lubbock

It does not take much strength to do things, but it requires great strength to decide on what to do.
Elbert Hubbard

Living is a constant process of deciding what we are going to do.
José Ortega y Gasset

Think like a man of action, act like a man of thought.
Henry Bergson

We are our choices.
Jean-Paul Sartre

democracy ⚉

The purpose of a democratic society is to make great persons.
Lyman Bryson

The test of democracy is freedom of criticism.
David Ben-Gurion

details ⚉

Beware of the man who won't be bothered with details.
William Feather

The savage in man is never quite eradicated.

Henry David Thoreau

All practical teachers know that education is a patient process of the mastery of details, minute by minute, hour by hour, day by day.

Alfred North Whitehead

discipline ॐ

To expect to rule others by assuming a loud tone is like thinking oneself tall by putting on high heels.

J. Petit-Senn

Discipline of the school should proceed from the life of the school as a whole and not directly from the teacher.

John Dewey

Make the work interesting and the discipline will take care of itself.

E. B. White

Students who act unmotivated, uncooperative, defiant, or irresponsible are discouraged human beings.

Robert Martin

The dominant note of education at its beginning and at its end is freedom, but . . . there is an intermediate stage of discipline with freedom in subordination.

Alfred North Whitehead

The "good" child may be frightened, and insecure, wanting only to please his parents by submitting to their will, while the "bad" child may have a will of his own and genuine interests but ones which do not please the parents.

Erich Fromm

33

discovery ॐ

From the very beginning of his education, the child should experience the joy of discovery.
Alfred North Whitehead

Discovery consists of seeing what everybody has seen and thinking what nobody has thought.
Albert Szent-Györgyi

It is by logic that we prove, but by intuition that we discover. To know how to criticize is good, but to know how to create is better.
Henri Poincaré

One of the advantages of being disorderly is that one is constantly making exciting discoveries.
A. A. Milne

There is always more chance of hitting upon something valuable when you aren't too sure what you want to hit upon.
Alfred North Whitehead

discussion & debate ॐ

Discussion is an exchange of knowledge; argument an exchange of ignorance.
Robert Quillen

He who knows only his own side of the case knows little of that.
John Stuart Mill

How many a dispute could have been deflated into a single paragraph if the disputants had dared to define their terms.
Aristotle

Keep cool; anger is not an argument.
Daniel Webster

The best argument is that which seems merely an explanation.

Dale Carnegie

(Ridicule is) the first and last argument of fools.

C. Simmons

To say the right thing at the right time, keep still most of the time.

John Roper

When everyone is against you, it means that you are absolutely wrong—or absolutely right.

Albert Guinon

doubt ঙ

Freedom of speech and freedom of action are meaningless without freedom to think. And there is no freedom of thought without doubt.

Bergen Evans

Doubt is not a pleasant mental state but certainty is a ridiculous one.

Voltaire

Doubt is what gets you an education.

Wilson Mizner

If you would be a real seeker after truth, it is necessary that at least once in your life you doubt, as far as possible, all things.

René Descartes

In all affairs it's a healthy thing now and then to hang a question mark on the things you have long taken for granted.

Bertrand Russell

Learning learns but one lesson: doubt!

George Bernard Shaw

dreaming ঙ

I have learned this at least by my experiment: that if one advances confidently in the direction of his dreams, and endeavors to live the life which he has imagined, he will meet with a success unexpected in common hours.

Henry David Thoreau

I like the dreams of the future better than the history of the past.

Thomas Jefferson

It may be those who do most, dream most.

Stephen Leacock

education ঙ

Education is not received. It is *achieved.*

Anonymous

All who have meditated on the art of governing mankind have been convinced that the fate of empires depends on the education of youth.

Aristotle

An educated man is one who can entertain a new idea, entertain another person, and entertain himself.

Sydney Herbert Wood

Education. That which discloses to the wise and disguises from the foolish their lack of understanding.

Ambrose Bierce

Education is the ability to listen to almost anything without losing your temper or your self-confidence.

Robert Frost

(Education is) what remains when we have forgotten all that we have been taught.

George Savile

Education makes a people easy to lead, but difficult to drive; easy to govern, but impossible to enslave.

Lord Brougham

Education should include knowledge of what to do with it.

Anonymous

I have never let my schooling interfere with my education.

Mark Twain

Let early education be a sort of amusement; you will then be better able to find out the natural bent.

Plato

It is because of our unassailable enthusiasm, our profound reverence for education, that we habitually demand of it the impossible. The teacher is expected to perform a choice and varied series of miracles.

Agnes Repplier

The central aim of education is to develop rational men who do not sin against themselves and their kind.

John Goodlad

The primary purpose of a liberal education is to make one's mind a pleasant place in which to spend one's leisure.

Sydney Harris

The school is the last expenditure upon which America should be willing to economize.

Franklin D. Roosevelt

There is a grave defect in the school where the playground suggests *happy* and the classroom *disagreeable* thoughts.

John Spalding

37

When you get into a tight place and everything goes against you, till it seems you could not hold on a minute longer, never give up then for that is just the place and time that the tide will turn.

Harriet Beecher Stowe

To be able to be caught up into the world of thought—that is being educated.

Edith Hamilton

To learn is to change. Education is a process that changes the learner.

George Leonard

What is learned in high school, or for that matter anywhere at all, depends far less on what is taught than on what one actually experiences in the place.

Edgar Friedenberg

What is really important in education is not that the child learns this and that, but that the mind is matured, that energy is aroused.

Søren Kierkegaard

effort &

And thou wilt give thyself relief, if thou doest every act of thy life as if it were the last.

Marcus Aurelius

Nothing got without pains but an ill name and long nails.

Scottish proverb

What is easy and obvious is never valued; and even what is in itself difficult, if we come to the knowledge of it without difficulty, and without any stretch of thought or judgment, is but little regarded.

David Hume

encouragement &

Keep away from people who try to belittle your ambitions. Small people always do that, but the really great make you feel that you, too, can become great.

Mark Twain

39

I now perceive one immense omission in my *Psychology*—the deepest principle of human nature is the craving to be appreciated.
William James

Taking an interest in what students are thinking and doing is often a much more powerful form of encouragement than praise.
Robert Martin

Every misbehaving child is discouraged and needs continuous encouragement, just as a plant needs water and sunshine.
Rudolf Dreikurs

enemies ❧

A tough lesson in life that one has to learn is that not everybody wishes you well.
Dan Rather

A wise man gets more use from his enemies than a fool from his friends.
Baltasar Gracián

He that wrestles with us strengthens our nerves and sharpens our skill. Our antagonist is our helper.
Edmund Burke

Love your enemies, for they tell you your faults.
Benjamin Franklin

enthusiasm ❧

A man can succeed at almost anything for which he has unlimited enthusiasm.
Charles Schwab

Enthusiasm is contagious—and so is the lack of it.
Anonymous

Every great and commanding moment in the annals of the world is the triumph of some enthusiasm.
Ralph Waldo Emerson

Those who have no fire in themselves cannot warm others.
Anonymous

I don't know if I should care for a man who made life easy; I should want someone who made it interesting.
Edith Wharton

In the ideal sense nothing is uninteresting; there are only uninterested people.
Brooks Atkinson

When you are genuinely interested in one thing, it will always lead to something else.
Eleanor Roosevelt

ethics ⚮

Do not envy a sinner; you don't know what disaster awaits him.
The Bible

If you would convince a man that he does wrong, do right. Men will believe what they see.
Henry David Thoreau

The only good is knowledge and the only evil is ignorance.
Socrates

evaluation ⚮

I get quiet joy from the observation of anyone who does his job well.
William Feather

No instrument smaller than the world is fit to measure men and women: Examinations measure Examinees.

Sir Walter Raleigh

Every man is entitled to be valued by his best moments.
Ralph Waldo Emerson

As I grow older, I pay less attention to what men say. I just watch what they do.
Andrew Carnegie

At the day of judgment we shall not be asked what we have read but what we have done.
Thomas a Kempis

Don't judge anyone harshly until you yourself have been through his experiences.
Goethe

He is well onward in the way of wisdom who can bear a reproof and mend by it.
Proverb

I do not believe that gifts, whether of mind or character, can be weighed like butter and sugar, not even at Cambridge.
Virginia Woolf

Look for the good things, not the faults. It takes a good deal bigger-sized brain to find out what is not wrong with people and things, than to find out what is wrong.
R. L. Sharpe

Men are not to be judged by what they do not know, but by what they do know, and the manner in which they know it.
Vauvenargues

There is probably an element of malice in our readiness to over-estimate people—we are, as it were, laying up for ourselves the pleasure of later cutting them down to size.
Eric Hoffer

Think not those faithful who praise all thy words
and actions; but those who kindly reprove thy
faults.
Socrates

To sensible men, every day is a day of reckoning.
John Gardner

We measure the excellency of other men by some
excellency we conceive to be in ourselves.
John Selden

We praise or blame according to whether the one or
the other offers a great opportunity for our power of
judgment to shine out.
Friedrich Nietzsche

examples ❧

A good example has twice the value of good advice.
Anonymous

Example is not the main thing in life—it is the only
thing.
Albert Schweitzer

Example is the school of mankind, and they will
learn at no other.
Edmund Burke

It is difficult to inspire others to accomplish what
you haven't been willing to try.
Anonymous

Teachers teach more by what they are than by what
they say.
Anonymous

exams ❧

No instrument smaller than the world is fit to mea-
sure men and women: Examinations measure
Examinees.
Sir Walter Raleigh

To treat your facts with imagination is one thing, to imagine your facts is another.

John Burroughs

excellence ✃

If you would be remembered, do one thing superbly well.

Saunders Norvell

One of the rarest things that a man ever does is to do the best he can.

Josh Billings

To get the best out of a man, go to what is best in him.

Daniel Considine

Man is the only animal that laughs and weeps; for he is the only animal that is struck with the difference between what things are, and what they ought to be.

William Hazlitt

excuses ✃

Don't do what you'll have to find an excuse for.

Anonymous

And oftentimes excusing of a fault
Doth make the fault the worse by the excuse.

William Shakespeare

He who excuses himself, accuses himself.

French proverb

It takes less time to do a thing right than it does to explain why you did it wrong.

Henry Wadsworth Longfellow

*Life is what we make it,
always has been, always
will be.*

Grandma Moses

Never give an excuse that you would not be willing to accept.

Anonymous

The person who really wants to do something finds a way; the other person finds an excuse.

Anonymous

experience 🦡

Nothing ever becomes real till it is experienced—even a proverb is no proverb to you till your life has illustrated it.

John Keats

Experience is a good teacher, but she sends in terrific bills.

Minna Antrim

All life is an experiment. The more experiments you make the better.

Ralph Waldo Emerson

Experience is not what happens to you; it is what you do with what happens to you.

Aldous Huxley

Experience teaches.

Tacitus

How vain it is to sit down to write when you have not stood up to live!

Henry David Thoreau

Life is a series of experiences, each one of which makes us bigger, even though sometimes it is hard to realize this.

Henry Ford

No, you never get any fun
Out of the things you haven't done.

Ogden Nash

The great difficulty in education is to get experience out of idea.

George Santayana

The one and only substitute for experience which we have not ourselves had is art, literature.

Aleksandr Solzhenitsyn

There are many truths of which the full meaning cannot be realized until personal experience has brought it home.

John Stuart Mill

To know the road ahead, ask those coming back.

Chinese proverb

explanations 🕸

I am the master of everything I can explain.

Theodore Haecker

I wish he would explain his explanation.

Lord Byron

facts 🕸

A fact in itself is nothing. It is valuable only for the idea attached to it, or for the proof which it furnishes.

Claude Bernard

"Now, what I want is facts. Teach these boys and girls nothing but facts. Facts alone are wanted in life. Plant nothing else, and root out everything else. You can only for the mind of reasoning animals depend upon facts: nothing else will ever be of any service to them. This is the principle on which I bring up these children. Stick to facts, sir!"

Charles Dickens

Be obscure clearly.

E. B. White

Sit down before fact as a little child, be prepared to give up every preconceived notion, follow humbly wherever and to whatever abysses nature leads, or you shall learn nothing.
Thomas Huxley

The frontiers are not east or west, north or south, but wherever a man *fronts* a fact.
Henry David Thoreau

The office of the scholar is to cheer, to raise, and to guide men by showing them facts amidst appearances.
Ralph Waldo Emerson

faculty meetings ༚

Opinions cannot survive if one has no chance to fight for them.
Thomas Mann

To say nothing, especially when speaking, is half the art of diplomacy.
Will and Ariel Durant

You'll find in no park or city,
A monument to a committee.
Victoria Pasternak

How come nobody wants to argue with me? Is it because I'm always so right?
Jim Bouton

failure ༚

Notice the difference between what happens when a man says to himself, "I have failed three times," and what happens when he says, "I am a failure."
S. I. Hayakawa

The prime purpose of eloquence is to keep other people from speaking.

Louis Vermeil

Failure is, in a sense, the highway to success, inasmuch as every discovery of what is false leads us to seek earnestly after what is true.

John Keats

(Failure is) only the opportunity to begin again, more intelligently.

Henry Ford

I cannot give you the formula for success, but I can give you the formula for failure—which is: Try to please everybody.

Herbert Swope

The probability that we shall fail in the struggle should not deter us from the support of a cause we believe to be just.

Abraham Lincoln

There is no failure except in no longer trying.

Elbert Hubbard

This thing that we call "failure" is not the falling down, but the staying down.

Mary Pickford

fame

Fame is proof that people are gullible.

Ralph Waldo Emerson

When the million applaud, you should ask yourself what harm you have done; when they censure you, what good.

Charles Caleb Colton

An expert is a person from another city; the farther away the city, the greater the expert.

Anonymous

The fame of great men ought always to be estimated by the means used to acquire it.

Anonymous

fear ⚘

Even in the kindest and gentlest of schools, children are afraid, many of them a great deal of the time, some of them almost all of the time. This is a hard fact to deal with. What can we do about it?
John Holt

(Fear is) nature's warning signal to get busy.
Henry C. Link

Fear is the darkroom where negatives are developed.
Anonymous

Keep your fears to yourself, but share your courage with others.
Robert Louis Stevenson

field trips ⚘

In traveling, a man must carry knowledge with him if he would bring home knowledge.
Dr. Johnson

My favorite thing is to go where I've never been.
Diane Arbus

fighting ⚘

Never corner an opponent, and always assist him to save his face.
B. H. Liddell Hart

The best armor is to keep out of range.
Proverb

flattery ⚘

We recognize that flattery is poison, but its perfume intoxicates us.
Marquis De La Grande

What flatterers say, try to make true.
German proverb

friendship 🎴

The only way to have a friend is to be one.
Ralph Waldo Emerson

True friendship comes when silence between two people is comfortable.
Dave Gentry

(A friend is) one who knows all about you and loves you just the same.
Elbert Hubbard

Associate yourself with men of good quality if you esteem your own reputation for 'tis better to be alone than in bad company.
George Washington

Be civil to all; sociable to many; familiar with few; friend to one; enemy to none.
Benjamin Franklin

Friendship is like health: its value is seldom known until it is lost.
Anonymous

Go often to the house of thy friend; for weeds soon choke up the unused path.
Scandinavian proverb

Hear no ill of a friend, nor speak any of an enemy.
Benjamin Franklin

If I knew for a certainty that a man was coming to my house with the conscious design of doing me good, I should run for my life.
Henry David Thoreau

The essential charm of good talking rests upon sincerity, spontaneity, and the willing revelation of character.

John Hobbes

If it's very painful for you to criticize your friends—
you're safe in doing it. But if you take the slightest
pleasure in it—that's the time to hold your tongue.
Alice Duer Miller

If you have one true friend, you have more than
your share comes to.
Thomas Fuller

Probably no man ever had a friend that he did not
dislike a little.
E. W. Howe

Seek not every quality in one individual.
Confucius

The golden rule of friendship is to listen to others as
you would have them listen to you.
David Augsburger

A friend is a person with whom I may be sincere.
Before him, I may think aloud.
Ralph Waldo Emerson

When a friend is in trouble, don't annoy him by
asking if there is anything you can do. Think up
something appropriate and do it.
E. W. Howe

You can hardly make a friend in a year, but you can
lose one in an hour.
Chinese proverb

future ᔰ

Fear of the future is a waste of the present.
Anonymous

Whatever your past has been, you have a spotless
future.
Anonymous

genius ஃ

Genius means little more than the faculty of perceiving in an unhabitual way.
William James

Genius does what it must, talent does what it can.
Edward Bulwer-Lytton

Genius is the ability to reduce the complicated to the simple.
C. W. Ceram

It is the essence of genius to make use of the simplest ideas.
Charles Peguy

Men give me credit for genius; but all the genius I have lies in this: When I have a subject on hand, I study it profoundly.
Alexander Hamilton

The function of genius is not to give new answers, but pose new questions which time and mediocrity can resolve.
H. R. Trevor-Roper

When a true genius appears in the world, you may know him by this sign, that the dunces are all in confederacy against him.
Jonathan Swift

goals ஃ

First say to yourself what you would be; and then do what you have to do.
Epictetus

A man should have any number of little aims about which he should be conscious and for which he should have names, but he should have neither name for, nor consciousness concerning, the main aim of his life.
Samuel Butler

Ah, but a man's reach should exceed his grasp
Or what's a heaven for?

Robert Browning

Before we set our hearts too much on anything, let
us examine how happy are those who already possess it.

La Rochefoucauld

Continuity of purpose is one of the most essential
ingredients of happiness in the long run, and for
most men this comes chiefly through their work.

Bertrand Russell

Great minds have purposes, others have wishes.

Washington Irving

He who would leap high must take a long run.

Proverb

One half of knowing what you want is knowing
what you must give up before you get it.

Sidney Howard

The significance of man is not in what he attains, but
in what he longs to attain.

Albert Schweitzer

Without some goal and some effort to reach it, no
man can live.

Fyodor Dostoevski

gossip &

If you hear that someone is speaking ill of you,
instead of trying to defend yourself you should say:
"He obviously does not know me very well, since
there are so many other faults he could have
mentioned."

Epictetus

Never tell evil of a man, if you do not know it for a certainty, and if you know it for a certainty, then ask yourself, "Why should I tell it?"

Johann K. Lavater

(Rumor is) a favorite weapon of the assassins of character.

Ambrose Bierce

To speak ill of others is a dishonest way of praising ourselves.

Will and Ariel Durant

Whoever gossips *to* you will gossip *about* you.

Spanish proverb

growing up &

One stops being a child when one realizes that telling one's trouble does not make it better.

Cesare Pavese

A child becomes an adult when he realizes he has a right not only to be right but also to be wrong.

Thomas Szasz

Children can't grow if they're not allowed to make their own decisions.

Anonymous

habits &

The unfortunate thing about this world is that good habits are so much easier to give up than bad ones.

W. Somerset Maugham

Cultivate only the habits that you are willing should master you.

Elbert Hubbard

Each year one vicious habit rooted out,
In time might make the worst man good
  throughout.
Benjamin Franklin

The chains of habit are too weak to be felt until they
are too strong to be broken.
Dr. Johnson

Wise living consists perhaps less in acquiring good
habits than in acquiring as few habits as possible.
Eric Hoffer

happiness ⚜

This is the true joy in life, the being used for a
purpose recognized by yourself as a mighty one.
George Bernard Shaw

It is one of my sources of happiness never to desire a
knowledge of other people's business.
Dolly Madison

Life owes us little; we owe it everything. The only
true happiness comes from squandering ourselves
for a purpose.
John Mason Brown

Most folks are about as happy as they make up their
minds to be.
Abraham Lincoln

On the whole, the happiest people seem to be those
who have no particular cause for being happy
except that they are so.
William Inge

Some pursue happiness—others create it.
Anonymous

When one door of happiness closes another opens;
but often we look so long at the closed door that we
do not see the one which has been opened for us.
Helen Keller

The best preparation for being a happy and useful man or woman is to live fully as a child.

Plowden Report

hatred ⊠

Always remember others may hate you, but those who hate you don't win unless you hate them.
Richard Nixon

Hating people is like burning down your own house to get rid of a rat.
Harry Fosdick

Never in this world can hatred be stilled by hatred.
Buddha

heroes ⊠

Being a hero is about the shortest-lived profession on earth.
Will Rogers

Heroism consist in hanging on one minute longer.
Norwegian proverb

Self-trust is the essence of heroism.
Ralph Waldo Emerson

There is not a more unhappy being than a superannuated idol.
Joseph Addison

We can't all be heroes because someone has to sit on the curb and clap as they go by.
Will Rogers

history ⊠

Not to know the events which happened before one was born, that is to remain always a boy.
Cicero

Our ignorance of history makes us libel our own times. People have always been like this.
Gustav Flaubert

Political history is far too criminal and pathological to be a fit subject of study for the young. Children should acquire their heroes and villains from fiction.
W. H. Auden

The only thing we learn from history is that we do not learn.
Earl Warren

The only use of a knowledge of the past is to equip us for the present. No more deadly harm can be done to young minds than by depreciation of the present. The present contains all that there is. It is holy ground; for it is the past, and it is the future.
Alfred North Whitehead

honesty ⚮

There are no degrees of honesty.
Anonymous

Prefer loss to the wealth of dishonest gain; the former vexes you for a time; the latter will bring you lasting remorse.
Chilo

So live your life that your autograph will be wanted instead of your fingerprints.
Anonymous

The person who is straightforward and honest doesn't have to worry about a faulty memory.
Anonymous

honors ⚮

It is better to deserve honors and not have them than to have them and not deserve them.
Mark Twain

Dignity does not consist in possessing honors, but in deserving them.

Aristotle

Prizes bring bad luck. Academic prizes, prizes for virtue, decorations, all these inventions of the devil encourage hypocrisy, and freeze the spontaneous upsurge of a free heart.

Charles Baudelaire

humanity

Human nature is ever capable of improvement and never able of being made perfect.

John Clare

I know of no rights of race superior to the rights of humanity.

Frederick Douglass

In each of us there is a little of all of us.

Georg Lichtenberg

We are healthy only to the extent that our ideas are humane.

Kurt Vonnegut

You must not lose faith in humanity. Humanity is an ocean; if a few drops of the ocean are dirty, the ocean does not become dirty.

Mohandas Gandhi

ideas

Don't despair of a student if he has one clear idea.

Nathanial Emmons

Nothing is more dangerous than an idea, when it's the only one we have.

Émile Chartier

One of the greatest pains to human nature is the
pain of a new idea.
Walter Bagehot

The best ideas are common property.
Seneca

The finest thought runs the risk of being irretriev-
ably forgotten if it is not written down.
Arthur Schopenhauer

Very simple ideas are within the reach of only very
complicated minds.
Remy De Gourmont

What matters is not the idea a man holds, but the
depth at which he holds it.
Ezra Pound

ignorance ❧

A man with little learning is like the frog who thinks
its puddle a great sea.
Proverb

Being ignorant is not so much a shame, as being
unwilling to learn.
Benjamin Franklin

Everybody is ignorant, only on different subjects.
Will Rogers

Genuine ignorance is...profitable because it is
likely to be accompanied by humility, curiosity, and
open-mindedness; whereas ability to repeat catch-
phrases, cant terms, familiar propositions, gives the
conceit of learning and coats the mind with varnish
waterproof to new ideas.
John Dewey

I have never met a man so ignorant that I couldn't
learn something from him.
Galileo Galilei

*I shut my eyes in order
to see.*
Paul Gauguin

It is better to know nothing than to know what ain't so.

H. W. Shaw

Thinking you know when in fact you don't is a fatal mistake, to which we are all prone.

Bertrand Russell

(Ignorance is) the mother of fear.

Nicholas Ling

To be ignorant of one's ignorance is the malady of ignorance.

A. Bronson Alcott

Wise men learn more from fools than fools from wise men.

Cato

imagination ⅗

Imagination is more important than knowledge.

Albert Einstein

Imagination, not invention, is the supreme master of art as of life.

Joseph Conrad

This world is but canvas to our imaginations.

Henry David Thoreau

To know is nothing at all; to imagine is everything.

Anatole France

impatience ⅗

Impatience is waiting in a hurry.

Anonymous

Like farmers we need to learn that we can't sow and reap on the same day.

Anonymous

*It may be those who
do most, dream most.*

Stephen Leacock

About the only thing you can get without patience is impatience.

Anonymous

impossibilities

The impossible is often the untried.

Jim Goodwin

Impossibility is a word only to be found in the dictionary of fools.

Napoleon Bonaparte

An impossibility does not disturb us until its accomplishment shows what fools we were.

Henry Haskins

I cannot discover that anyone knows enough to say definitely what is and what is not possible.

Henry Ford

Sometimes I've believed as many as six impossible things before breakfast.

Lewis Carroll

independence

The best thing we can do for those we love is to help them escape from us.

Baron Friedrich von Hügel

The man who goes alone can start today; but he who travels with another must wait till that other is ready.

Henry David Thoreau

individual differences

The most universal quality is diversity.

Montaigne

*A man must consider
what a rich realm
he abdicates when he
becomes a conformist.*

Ralph Waldo Emerson

The society of sheep must in time beget a government of wolves.

Bertrand de Jouvenel

But the great Master said, "I see
No best in kind, but in degree;
I gave a various gift to each,
To charm, to strengthen, and to teach."

Henry Wadsworth Longfellow

Commandment Number One of any truly civilized society is this: Let people be different.

David Grayson

Even in ordinary social intercourse the most delicate compliment is to treat the person with whom you are talking as an exception to all rules.

Samuel Crothers

Many great things indeed have been achieved by those who chose not to leap into the mainstream.

Joan Mondale

If a man does not keep pace with his companions, perhaps it is because he hears a different drummer. Let him step to the music which he hears, however measured or far away.

Henry David Thoreau

The shoe that fits one person pinches another; there is no recipe for living that suits all cases.

Carl Jung

There lurks...in every human heart a desire of distinction which inclines every man first to hope, and then to believe, that nature has given him something peculiar to himself.

Dr. Johnson

Which can say more than this rich praise—that you alone are you.

William Shakespeare

initiative ❧

If there is no wind, row.
Latin proverb

(Initiative is) doing the right thing without being told.
Elbert Hubbard

It is the greatest of all mistakes to do nothing because you can do only a little. Do what you can.
Sydney Smith

intellectuals ❧

A country without intellectuals is like a body without a head.
Ayn Rand

intelligence ❧

In the conditions of modern life the rule is absolute: the race which does not value trained intelligence is doomed.
Alfred North Whitehead

A man is not necessarily intelligent because he has plenty of ideas, anymore than he is a good general because he has plenty of soldiers.
Nicolas Chamfort

An intelligent person not only knows how to take advice, but also how to reject it.
Anonymous

Curiosity is nothing more than freewheeling intelligence.
Anonymous

Intelligence is quickness in seeing things as they are.
George Santayana

There is no limit to intelligence...or to ignorance.
Anonymous

judgment ✣

Everyone complains of his memory, and no one complains of his judgment.
La Rochefoucauld

The supreme end of education is expert discernment in all things—the power to tell the good from the bad, the genuine from the counterfeit, and to prefer the good and the genuine to the bad and the counterfeit.
Dr. Johnson

kindness ✣

Kindness begets kindness.
Sophocles

Be pleasant until ten o'clock in the morning and the rest of the day will take care of itself.
Elbert Hubbard

Flowers leave some of their fragrance in the hand that bestows them.
Chinese proverb

Forget injuries, never forget kindnesses.
Confucius

Teach me to feel another's woe.
Alexander Pope

knowledge ✣

Knowledge and human power are synonymous.
Francis Bacon

All knowledge is of itself of some value. There is nothing so minute or inconsiderable, that I would not rather know it than not.

Dr. Johnson

If a little knowledge is dangerous, where is the man who has so much as to be out of danger?

Thomas Huxley

If you have knowledge, let others light their candles at it.

Margaret Fuller

If the school sends out children with a desire for knowledge and some idea of how to acquire and use it, it will have done its work.

Sir Richard Livingstone

Knowing without doing is like plowing without sowing.

Anonymous

Knowledge, like lumber, is best when well-seasoned.

Anonymous

More and more, I used the quickness of my mind to pick the minds of other people and use their knowledge as my own.

Eleanor Roosevelt

Most students treat knowledge as a liquid to be swallowed rather than as a solid to be chewed, and then wonder why it provides so little nourishment.

Sydney Harris

No one sees further into a generalization than his own knowledge of details extends.

William James

Not to know is bad; not to wish to know is worse.

African proverb

Free every Monday through Friday—knowledge.
Bring your own containers.

Sign on a high school bulletin board
in Dallas, Texas

The more one penetrates the realm of knowledge,
the more puzzling everything becomes.

Henry Miller

Tim was so learned, that he could name a horse in
nine languages. So ignorant, that he bought a cow to
ride on.

Benjamin Franklin

We don't know one millionth of one percent about
anything.

Thomas Edison

What is more wonderful than the delight which the
mind feels when it *knows?* This delight is not for
anything beyond the knowing, but is in the act of
knowing. It is the satisfaction of a primary instinct.

Mark Rutherford

language ஜ

The limits of my language stand for the limits of my
world.

Ludwig Wittgenstein

laughter & humor ஜ

(Humor is) the sunshine of the mind.

Edward Bulwer-Lytton

A very wise old teacher once said: "I consider a
day's teaching is wasted if we do not all have one
hearty laugh." He meant that when people laugh
together, they cease to be young and old, master
and pupils, workers and driver, jailer and prisoners,
they become a single group of human beings enjoy-
ing its existence.

Gilbert Highet

Men show their character in nothing more clearly than by what they think laughable.
Goethe

Of all days, the day on which one has not laughed is surely the most wasted.
Nicolas Chamfort

With the fearful strain that is on me night and day, if I did not laugh I should die.
Abraham Lincoln

leadership ⚜

It is extremely difficult to lead farther than you have gone yourself.
Anonymous

If you wish to know what a man is, place him in authority.
Yugoslav proverb

Education can't make us all leaders, but it can teach us which leader to follow.
Anonymous

The final test of a leader is that he leaves behind him in other men the conviction and the will to carry on.
Walter Lippmann

What you cannot enforce, do not command.
Sophocles

learning ⚜

If we succeed in giving the love of learning, the learning itself is sure to follow.
John Lubbock

All students can learn.
Christopher Morley

Learning is not child's play; we cannot learn without pain.
Aristotle

Learning is the discovery that something is possible.
Fritz Perls

Learning makes a man fit company for himself.
Thomas Fuller

People in school today can expect a lifetime in which knowledge itself will radically change—not only in its details but in its structures; so that the mark of a truly educated man will no longer be how much or even how variously he knows, but how quickly and how completely he can continually learn.
Richard Kostelanetz

Some people will never learn anything, for this reason: because they understand everything too soon.
Alexander Pope

The man who is too old to learn was probably always too old to learn.
Henry Haskins

There are no easy methods of learning difficult things; the method is to close your door: give out that you are not at home, and work.
Joseph de Maistre

Whoever cares to learn will always find a teacher.
German proverb

You come to know a thing by being inside it.
Edmund Carpenter

lesson plans ఞ

Never take anything for granted.
Benjamin Disraeli

77

When resting in safety, do not forget that danger may come.
Confucius

Truly nothing is to be expected but the unexpected.
Alice James

Seize from every moment its unique novelty and do not prepare your joys.
André Gide

If life were predictable, it would cease to be life and be without flavor.
Eleanor Roosevelt

library &

A library is a hospital for the mind.
Anonymous

Don't join the book burners . . . Don't be afraid to go in your library and read every book.
Dwight D. Eisenhower

Books are not made for furniture, but there is nothing else that so beautifully furnishes a house.
Henry Ward Beecher

A man should keep his little brain attic stocked with all the furniture that he is likely to use, and the rest he can put away in the lumber-room of his library, where he can get it if he wants it.
Arthur Conan Doyle

life &

Life is what we make it, always has been, always will be.
Grandma Moses

The trouble with facts is that there are so many of them.

Samuel Crothers

Fear not that life shall come to an end, but rather fear that it shall never have a beginning.

Cardinal Joseph Newman

It is while you are patiently toiling at the little tasks of life that the meaning and shape of the great whole of life dawn on you.

Phillips Brooks

Pythagoras used to say life resembles the Olympic Games; a few men strain their muscles to carry off a prize; others bring trinkets to sell to the crowd for a profit; and some there are (and not the worst) who seek no further advantage than to look at the show and see how and why everything is done. They are spectators of other men's lives in order to better judge and manage their own.

Montaigne

The life of every man is a diary in which he means to write one story and writes another; and his humblest hour is when he compares the volume as it is with what he vowed to make.

J. M. Barrie

The life so short, the craft so long to learn.

Hippocrates

The tragedy of life is not so much what men suffer, but rather what they miss.

Thomas Carlyle

listening ⚞

When people talk, listen completely. Most people never listen.

Ernest Hemingway

From listening comes wisdom, and from speaking repentance.

Italian proverb

He understands badly who listens badly.
Welsh proverb

Know how to listen, and you will profit even from those who talk badly.
Plutarch

One of the best ways to persuade others is with your ears—by listening to them.
Dean Rusk

There is only one rule for being a good talker—learn how to listen.
Christopher Morley

While the right to talk may be the beginning of freedom, the necessity of listening is what makes that right important.
Walter Lippmann

You can't fake listening. It shows.
Raquel Welch

love ⚬

Children need love, especially when they do not deserve it.
Harold Hulbert

Love is saying "I feel differently" instead of "You're wrong."
Anonymous

Love is the active concern for the life and growth of that which we love.
Erich Fromm

Hate the sin and love the sinner.
Mohandas Gandhi

luck ⚬

Be grateful for luck, but don't depend on it.
William Feather

*From the very beginning
of his education, the
child should experience
the joy of discovery.*

Alfred North Whitehead

Chance favors the prepared mind.
Louis Pasteur

Life is so largely controlled by chance that its conduct can be but a perpetual improvisation.
W. Somerset Maugham

manners ✂

Good manners and soft words have brought many a difficult thing to pass.
John Vanbrough

Manners are the happy ways of doing things.
Ralph Waldo Emerson

Rudeness is a weak man's imitation of strength.
Eric Hoffer

materials ✂

If you want to see what children can do, you must stop giving them things.
Norman Douglas

Keep a thing seven years and it's bound to come in handy.
Russian proverb

Only when children have had time to play and explore new materials in their own way will they be able to see the materials as learning materials.
Mary Baratta-Lorton

mathematics ✂

Accuracy, being able to figure out the correct answer consistently, is...more important than speed.
Mary Baratta-Lorton

Mathematics is the only science where one never knows what one is talking about, nor whether what is said is true.

Bertrand Russell

A mathematician, like a painter or a poet, is a maker of patterns.

G. H. Hardy

There is not a royal road to geometry.

Euclid

memory ॐ

Memory is the art of attention.

Dr. Johnson

Education means developing the mind, not stuffing the memory.

Anonymous

I doubt if anything learnt at school is of more value than great literature learnt by heart.

Sir Richard Livingstone

It is the memory that enables a person to gather roses in January.

Anonymous

(Memory is) the library of the mind.

Francis Fauvel-Gourand

metaphor ॐ

The metaphor is probably the most fertile power possessed by man.

José Ortega y Gasset

mistakes ॐ

There is nothing final about a mistake, except its being taken as final.

Phyllis Bottome

This thing that we call
"failure" is not the falling
down, but the staying down.

Mary Pickford

Everyone makes mistakes. It is what you do afterwards that counts.
Anonymous

(A mistake is) evidence that somebody has tried to accomplish something.
John E. Babcock

A life spent in making mistakes is not only more honorable but more useful than a life spent in doing nothing.
George Bernard Shaw

A man should never be ashamed to own that he has been in the wrong, which is but saying, in other words, that he is wiser today than he was yesterday.
Jonathan Swift

During my life, I have often had to eat my own words, and on the whole I have found them a wholesome diet.
Winston Churchill

Give me a good fruitful error any time, full of seeds, bursting with its own corrections. You can keep your sterile truth for yourself.
Vilfredo Pareto

Knowledge rests not upon truth alone, but upon error also.
Carl Jung

Love truth, and pardon error.
Voltaire

Mistakes are their own instructors.
Horace

Only he who does nothing makes a mistake.
French proverb

People will listen a great deal more patiently while you explain your mistakes than when you explain your successes.
Wilbur Nesbit

When the most insignificant person tells us we are in error, we should listen, and examine ourselves, and see if it is so. To believe it possible we may be in error is the first step toward getting out of it.

Johann K. Lavater

When you make a mistake, don't look back at it long. Take the reason of the thing into your mind, and then look forward. Mistakes are lessons of wisdom. The past cannot be changed. The future is yet in your power.

Hugh White

motivation ஃ

The important thing is not so much that every child should be taught, as that every child should be given the wish to learn.

John Lubbock

A teacher who is attempting to teach without inspiring the pupil with a desire to learn is hammering on cold iron.

Horace Mann

Above all things we must take care that the child, who is not yet old enough to love his studies, does not come to hate them and dread the bitterness which he has once tasted, even when the years of infancy are left behind.

Marcus Fabius Quintilianus

If you have a loitering servant, place his dinner before him, and send him on an errand.

Spanish proverb

No knowledge is so easily found as when it is needed.

Robert Henri

That which anyone has been long learning unwillingly, he unlearns with proportional eagerness and haste.

William Hazlitt

The love of life is necessary to the vigorous prosecution of any undertaking.
Dr. Johnson

We strain hardest for things which are almost but not quite within our reach.
Frederick Faber

You must lead (people)...through self-interest. It is this alone that will keep them keyed up to the full capacity of their productiveness.
Charles H. Steinway

music &

Music expresses that which cannot be said and on which it is impossible to be silent.
Victor Hugo

(Music is) the only language in which you cannot say a mean or sarcastic thing.
John Erskine

noise &

An inability to stay quiet is one of the most conspicuous failings of mankind.
Walter Bagehot

observing &

All our knowledge has its origins in our perceptions.
Leonardo da Vinci

How are you going to see the sun if you lie on your stomach?
Ashanti proverb

It is only with the heart that one can see rightly; what is essential is invisible to the eye.
Antoine de Saint-Exupéry

Music resembles poetry; in each
Are nameless graces which no
methods teach.

Alexander Pope

My green thumb came only as a result of the mistakes I made while learning to see things from the plant's point of view.
H. Fred Ale

Somehow, if you really attend to the real, it tells you everything.
Robert Pollock

The first requirement for the growth of the individual is that the person remain in touch with his own perceptions.
Clark Moustakas

We read every day, with astonishment, things which we see every day without surprise.
Lord Chesterfield

We cannot create observers by saying "observe," but by giving them the power and the means for this observation, and these means are procured through education of the senses.
Maria Montessori

opinions ೫

Do not think of knocking out another person's brains because he differs in opinion from you. It would be as rational to knock yourself on the head because you differ from yourself ten years ago.
Horace Mann

Everyone has a right to his opinion, but no man has a right to be wrong about the facts.
Anonymous

A wise man gives other opinions as much weight as he does his own.
Anonymous

A foolish opinion shared by thousands is still a foolish opinion.
Anonymous

Error of opinion may be tolerated where reason is left free to combat it.
Thomas Jefferson

opportunities ᨸ

Opportunities are usually disguised as hard work, so most people don't recognize them.
Ann Landers

The great opportunity is where you are. Do not despise your own place and hour. Every place is under the stars, every place is the center of the world.
John Burroughs

There is no security on this earth; there is only opportunity.
Douglas MacArthur

When I look back now over my life and call to mind what I might have had simply for taking and did not take, my heart is like to break.
William Hale White

originality ᨸ

Original thoughts can be understood only in virtue of the unoriginal elements which they contain.
Stanislav Andreski

What is originality? To *see* something that has no name as yet and hence cannot be mentioned although it stares us all in the face. The way men usually are, it takes a name to make something visible for them. Those with originality have for the most part also assigned names.
Friedrich Nietzsche

paperwork

We can lick gravity, but sometimes the paperwork
is overwhelming.
Wernher von Braun

parents

The parent's life is the child's copy-book.
W. S. Partridge

The relation between parents and children is essentially based on teaching.
Gilbert Highet

Your children need your presence more than your
presents.
Jesse Jackson

Some parents could do more for their children by
not doing so much for them.
Anonymous

School life should grow gradually out of the home
life...it should take up and continue the activities
with which the child is already familiar in the home.
John Dewey

When I was a boy of 14, my father was so ignorant I
could hardly stand to have the old man around. But
when I got to be 21, I was astonished at how much
he had learned in seven years.
Mark Twain

Hold childhood in reverence and so not be in any
hurry to judge it for good or ill. Give nature time to
work before you take over the tasks, lest you interfere with her method.
Jean Jacques Rousseau

There are only two lasting bequests we can hope to give our children. One of these is roots; the other, wings.

Hodding Carter

What the best and wisest parent wants for his own child, that must the community want for all its children.

John Dewey

Before I got married, I had six theories about bringing up children; now I have six children and no theories.

John Wilmot

patience ✿

(Patience is) a necessary ingredient of genius.

Benjamin Disraeli

Only those who have the patience to do simple things perfectly will acquire the skill to do difficult things easily.

Johann von Schiller

Have patience with all things, but chiefly have patience with yourself.

Saint Francis de Sales

Patience is the best remedy for every trouble.

Plautus

perfection ✿

People who know their imperfections are just about as perfect as people can get.

Anonymous

persistence ✿

He conquers who endures.

Persius

Always at it wins the day.

Proverb

Great works are performed not by strength, but perseverance.

Dr. Johnson

Let me tell you the secret that has led me to my goal. My strength lies solely in my tenacity.

Louis Pasteur

Nothing great was ever done without much enduring.

Saint Catherine of Siena

One may go a long way after one is tired.

French proverb

When you get into a tight place and everything goes against you, till it seems you could not hold on a minute longer, never give up then for that is just the place and time that the tide will turn.

Harriet Beecher Stowe

Fall seven times, stand up eight.

Japanese proverb

physical education 🐚

Playing children are motivated primarily to enjoy living. This is the major rehearsal value of play and games, for without the ability to enjoy life, the long years of adulthood can be dull and wearisome.

Brian Sutton-Smith

There's lots of people who spend so much time watching their health, they haven't got time to enjoy it.

Josh Billings

Sedentary people are apt to have sluggish minds. A sluggish mind is apt to be reflected in flabbiness of body and in a dullness of expression that invites no interest and gets none.

Rose Fitzgerald Kennedy

Interest and proficiency in almost any
one activity—swimming, boating, fishing,
skiing, skating—breed interest in many
more. Once someone discovers the delight
of mastering one skill, however slightly,
he is likely to try out not just one more,
but a whole ensemble.

Margaret Mead

We teach you the pleasure of physical exercise—the team-spirit of games, too, for when you leave school finally you will find that life is a game, sometimes serious, sometimes fun, but a game that must be played with true team-spirit—there is no room for the outsider in life.
Shelagh Delaney

The only exercise some people get is running out of money.
Anonymous

poetry ⚘

You will never be alone with a poet in your pocket.
John Adams

Poetry is more philosophical and of greater importance than history.
Aristotle

Poetry is the language in which man explores his own amazement.
Christopher Fry

Poets utter great and wise things which they do not themselves understand.
Plato

popularity ⚘

A free society is one where it is safe to be unpopular.
Adlai Stevenson

(Popularity is) a crime from the moment it is sought; it is only a virtue where men have it whether they will or no.
Lord Halifax

Popularity is a form of success that is seldom worth the things you have to do in order to attain it.
Anonymous

practice &

More men become good through practice than by nature.
Democritus of Abdera

In all regions of life exercise strengthens capacity.
Anonymous

People always told me that my natural ability and good eyesight were the reasons for my success as a hitter. They never talk about the practice, practice, practice!
Ted Williams

When you are not practicing, remember, someone somewhere is practicing, and when you meet him he will win.
Ed Macauley

praise & rewards &

Both praise and criticism lead us to believe that someone can give us much more than he possesses.
Paul Valéry

Among the smaller duties of life I hardly know any one more important than that of not praising where praise is not due.
Sydney Smith

Do you want to injure someone's reputation? Don't speak ill of him, speak too well.
André Siegfried

Great tranquility of heart is his who cares for neither praise nor blame.
Thomas a Kempis

If we happen to be praised on account of qualities which we formerly despised, our estimation of those qualities immediately rises.

Giacomo Leopardi

None are more apt to praise others extravagantly than those who desire to be praised themselves.

Anonymous

Praises for our past triumphs are as feathers to a dead bird.

Paul Eldridge

The greater a man is, the more distasteful is praise and flattery to him.

John Burroughs

They say princes learn no art truly, but the art of horsemanship. The reason is, the brave beast is no flatterer. He will throw a prince as soon as his groom.

Ben Jonson

(Modesty is) the only sure bait when you angle for praise.

Lord Chesterfield

prejudice ౙ

In overcoming prejudice, working together is even more effective than talking together.

Ralph Sockman

It is never too late to give up our prejudices.

Henry David Thoreau

Never try to reason the prejudice out of a man. It was not reasoned into him, and cannot be reasoned out.

Sydney Smith

principals ଝ

Headmasters have powers at their disposal with which Prime Ministers have never yet been invested.

Winston Churchill

A good leader inspires people to have confidence in the leader; a great leader inspires people to have confidence in themselves.

Anonymous

As I would not be a slave, so I would not be a master. Whatever differs from this, to the extent of the difference, is no democracy.

Barbara Jordan

problem solving ଝ

Too often we give children answers to remember rather than problems to solve.

Roger Lewin

(A problem is) an opportunity in work clothes.

Henry J. Kaiser, Jr.

Every solution of a problem is a new problem.

Goethe

I had an immense advantage over many others dealing with the problem inasmuch as I had no fixed ideas derived from long established practice to control and bias my mind, and did not suffer from the general belief that whatever is, is right.

Henry Bessemer

The best way to escape from a problem is to solve it.

Brendan Francis

If you wish to know
what a man is, place
him in authority.

Yugoslav proverb

When I am working on a problem, I never think about beauty. I think only how to solve the problem. But when I have finished, if the solution is not beautiful, I know it is wrong.
Buckminster Fuller

procrastination ॐ

One today is worth two tomorrows.
Benjamin Franklin

It may be too late already, but it's not as much too late now as it will be later.
C. H. Weisert

Know the true value of time; snatch, seize, and enjoy every moment of it. No idleness; no laziness; no procrastination; never put off till tomorrow what you can do today.
Lord Chesterfield

Nothing is so fatiguing as the eternal hanging on of an uncompleted task.
William James

(Procrastination is) the father of failure.
Elbert Hubbard

Tomorrow is often the busiest day of the week.
Spanish proverb

What can be done at *any* time is never done at all.
English proverb

promises ॐ

Magnificent promises are always to be suspected.
Theodore Parker

Never promise more than you can perform.
Publilius Syrus

So teach us to number our days, that we may apply our hearts unto wisdom.

The Bible

PTA 🐝

A letter to the editor in response to a suggestion that teachers be kicked out of the PTA:

Editor:

We must not...take the "T" out of PTA. If we were to become the "Parent's Association" we would have only ourselves to blame for vandalism, low achievement, poor attendance, venereal disease outbreaks, pregnancies, and other social and emotional problems. We need our teachers. Without them we would have no scapegoats for the mess we've made of our present society.

Nancy Goebner

punishment 🐝

Distrust all in whom the impulse to punish is powerful.

Friedrich Nietzsche

People must never be humiliated—that is the main thing.

Anton Chekov

When a person praises punishment, nine times out of ten this means he is prepared to administer it rather than submit to it.

Anonymous

questions 🐝

If we would have new knowledge, we must get a whole world of new questions.

Susan Langer

A good question is never answered. It is not a bolt to be tightened into place but a seed to be planted and to bear more seed toward the hope of greening the landscape of idea.

John Ciardi

Better ask ten times than go astray once.
Proverb

Every question we answer leads on to another question. This has become the greatest survival trick of our species.
Desmond Morris

Judge people by their questions rather than by their answers.
Voltaire

(A young rabbi) went to the public schools and stood at the top of his class with little effort. He remembers vividly how his mother would tirelessly inquire, "Did you ask any good questions in school today?"
Frances Bellow

My greatest strength as a consultant is to be ignorant and ask a few questions.
Peter Drucker

Smart kids ask questions.
Marie Washington

The important thing is not to stop questioning.
Albert Einstein

The one real object of education is to have a man in the condition of continually asking questions.
Bishop Mandell Creighton

To be able to ask a question clearly is two-thirds of the way to getting it answered.
John Ruskin

The reward for working one's way through the known is to find a new question on the other side, formulated in a new way.
Jerome Bruner

reading ଙ୍

Reading is to the mind what exercise is to the body.
Richard Steele

Force yourself to reflect on what you read, paragraph by paragraph.
Samuel Taylor Coleridge

I divide all readers into two classes: Those who read to remember and those who read to forget.
William Phelps

I have often reflected upon the new vistas that reading opened to me. I knew right there in prison that reading had changed forever the course of my life. As I see it today, the ability to read awoke inside me some long dormant craving to be mentally alive.
Malcolm X

If we encounter a man of rare intellect, we should ask him what books he reads.
Ralph Waldo Emerson

In a very real sense, people who have read good literature have lived more than people who cannot or will not read.
S. I. Hayakawa

It is no more necessary that a man should remember the different dinners and suppers which have made him healthy, than the different books which have made him wise. Let us see the result of good food in a strong body, and the result of great reading in a full and powerful mind.
Sydney Smith

Let us read with method, and propose to ourselves an end to which our studies may point. The use of reading is to aid us in thinking.
Edward Gibbon

*There is more treasure
in books than in all
the pirate's loot on
Treasure Island.*

Walt Disney

Readers may be divided into four classes:

1. Sponges, who absorb all they read and return it nearly in the same state, only a little dirtied.
2. Sand-glasses, who retain nothing and are content to get through a book for the sake of getting through the time.
3. Strain-bags, who retain merely the dregs of what they read.
4. Mogul diamonds, equally rare and valuable, who profit by what they read, and enable others to profit by it also.

Samuel Taylor Coleridge

Resolve to edge in a little reading every day, if it is but a single sentence. If you gain fifteen minutes a day, it will make itself felt at the end of the year.

Horace Mann

The best effect of any book is that it excites the reader to self activity.

Thomas Carlyle

The way a book is read—which is to say, the qualities a reader brings to a book—can have as much to do with its worth as anything the author puts into it.

Norman Cousins

Those who don't read have no advantage over those who can't.

Anonymous

To acquire the habit of reading is to construct for yourself a refuge from almost all the miseries of life.

W. Somerset Maugham

To read without reflecting is like eating without digesting.

Edmund Burke

We shouldn't teach great books; we should teach a love of reading.

B. F. Skinner

The end of reading is not more books but more life.

Holbrook Jackson

recess ⚐

Take rest; a field that has rested gives a bountiful crop.

Ovid

Man is so made that he can only find relaxation from one kind of labor by taking up another.

Anatole France

Most sorts of diversion in men, children, and other animals, are an imitation of fighting.

Jonathan Swift

reform ⚐

It's always easy to reform the city—especially if you live in the country.

Anonymous

The pendulum of school reform swings between extremes of permissiveness and puritanical rule making, and tends to afflict generations alternatingly with the worst of both philosophies. But professional educators have an obligation to take a firmer stand against the absurdities of each fleeting era. It is in moderating the progressive and traditional extremes that the most promising answers may be found.

Fred Hechinger

report cards ⚐

I shall tell you a great secret, my friend. Do not wait for the last judgment. It takes place every day.

Albert Camus

An endeavor to please elders is at the bottom of high marks and mediocre careers.

John Chapman

To sit alone with my conscience will be judgment enough for me.

Charles Stubbs

responsibility ᔕ

A new position of responsibility will usually show a man to be a far stronger creature than was supposed.

William James

Few things help an individual more than to place responsibility upon him, and to let him know that you trust him.

Booker T. Washington

Responsibility for learning belongs to the student, regardless of age.

Robert Martin

Duty is the sublimest word in the language; you can never do more than your duty; you should never wish to do less.

Robert E. Lee

How can you come to know yourself? Never by thinking, always by doing. Try to do your duty, and you'll know right away what you amount to. And what is your duty? Whatever the day calls for.

Goethe

Make it a point to do something every day that you don't want to do. This is the golden rule for acquiring the habit of doing your duty without pain.

Mark Twain

Perhaps the most valuable result of all education is the ability to make yourself do the thing you have to do, when it ought to be done, whether you like it or not; it is the first lesson that ought to be learned; and however early a man's training begins, it is probably the last lesson that he learns thoroughly.

Thomas Huxley

We need to restore the full meaning of that old word, *duty*. It is the other side of rights.

Pearl Buck

revenge ஜ

He who injured you is either stronger or weaker. If he is weaker, spare him; if he is stronger, spare yourself.

Seneca

This is certain, that a man that studieth revenge keeps his wounds green, which otherwise would heal and do well.

Francis Bacon

risks ஜ

No noble thing can be done without risks.

Montaigne

One of the reasons mature people stop learning is that they become less and less willing to risk failure.

John Gardner

To win you have to risk loss.

Jean-Claude Killy

You may be disappointed if you fail, but you are doomed if you don't try.

Beverly Sills

The school is the last expenditure upon which America should be willing to economize.

Franklin D. Roosevelt

school 🦢

School is not preparation for life, but school *is* life.

John Dewey

Promote then as an object of primary importance, institutions for the general diffusion of knowledge. In proportion as the structure of government gives force to public opinion, it is essential that public opinion should be enlightened.

George Washington

School and education should not be confused; it is only school that can be made easy.

Anonymous

science 🦢

True science teaches, above all, to doubt and be ignorant.

Miguel de Unamuno y Jugo

Is ditch water dull? Naturalists with microscopes have told me that it teems with quiet fun.

G. K. Chesterton

It often happens that an unsuccessful experiment may produce an excellent observation. There are, therefore, no unsuccessful experiments.

Claude Bernard

Man has mounted science, and is now run away with. I firmly believe that before many centuries more, science will be the master of man. The engines he will have invented will be beyond his strength to control. Some day science may have the existence of mankind in its power, and the human race may commit suicide by blowing up the world.

Henry Adams

113

Science has promised us truth—an understanding of such relationships as our minds can grasp; it has never promised us either peace or happiness.

Gustav LeBon

The most incomprehensible thing about the world is that it is comprehensible.

Albert Einstein

Men love to wonder and that is the seed of our science.

Ralph Waldo Emerson

secrets

Three may keep a secret, if two of them are dead.

Benjamin Franklin

You can take better care of your secret than another can.

Ralph Waldo Emerson

self-confidence

(Self-confidence is) the first requisite to great undertakings.

Dr. Johnson

They are able because they think they are able.

Virgil

We lost because we told ourselves we lost.

Leo Tolstoy

Self-confidence is the memory of success.

Anonymous

self-control 🕸

Educate your children to self-control...and you have done much to abolish misery from their future lives and crimes from society.

Daniel Webster

The secret of all success is to know how to deny yourself. Prove that you can control yourself, and you are an educated man; and without this all other education is good for nothing.

R. D. Hitchcock

Whatever liberates our spirit without giving us mastery over ourselves is destructive.

Goethe

self-esteem 🕸

If a child lives with approval, he learns to live with himself.

Dorothy Nolte

A man who finds no satisfaction in himself, seeks for it in vain elsewhere.

La Rochefoucauld

If I despised myself, it would be no compensation if everyone saluted me, and if I respect myself, it does not trouble me if others hold me lightly.

Max Nordau

If you want to be respected, you must respect yourself.

Spanish proverb

It is a great mistake to fancy oneself greater than one is, and to value oneself at less than one is worth.

Goethe

self-knowledge &

Any sort of pretension induces mediocrity in art and life alike.
> *Margot Fonteyn*

Knowing your limitations is the first step toward overcoming them.
> *Anonymous*

Look well into thyself; there is a source of strength which will always spring up if thou wilt always look there.
> *Marcus Aurelius*

Man will become better only when you will make him see what he is like.
> *Anton Chekov*

Many a time I have wanted to stop talking and find out what I really believed.
> *Walter Lippmann*

Only the shallow know themselves.
> *Oscar Wilde*

Search others for their virtues, thyself for thy vices.
> *Benjamin Franklin*

We are so accustomed to wearing a disguise before others that eventually we are unable to recognize ourselves.
> *La Rochefoucauld*

We should every night call ourselves to an account: What infirmity have I mastered today? what passions opposed? what temptation resisted? what virtue acquired? Our vices will abate of themselves if they are brought every day to the shrift.
> *Seneca*

Know thyself.

Socrates

self-reliance &

No bird soars too high, if he soars with his own wings.
William Blake

As soon as you trust yourself, you will know how to live.
Goethe

If you want things to be right, you have to do them yourself.
Jacqueline Onassis

If you'd have it done, go. If not, send.
Benjamin Franklin

On the whole, we are meant to look after ourselves. It is certain each has to eat for himself, digest for himself, and in general care for his own dear life, and see to his own preservation; Nature's intentions, in most things uncertain, in this are decisive.
Arthur Clough

solitude &

People who cannot bear to be alone are generally the worst company.
Albert Guinon

I never found the companion that was so companionable as solitude. We are for the most part more lonely when we go abroad among men than when we stay in our chambers. A man thinking or working is always alone, let him be where he will.
Henry David Thoreau

One can acquire anything in solitude except character.
Stendhal

speechmaking ॐ

First learn the meaning of what you say, and then speak.

Epictetus

Always be shorter than anybody dared hope.

Lord Reading

It usually takes me more than three weeks to prepare a good impromptu speech.

Mark Twain

Always speak as though there were only one person in the hall whom you had to convince. Plead with him, argue with him, arouse him, touch him, but feel that your audience is one being whose confidence and affection you want to win.

Charles Reade

Be sincere; be brief; be seated.

Franklin D. Roosevelt

Make sure you have finished speaking before your audience has finished listening.

Dorothy Sarnoff

My basic rule is to speak slowly and simply so that my audience has an opportunity to follow and think about what I am saying.

Margaret Chase Smith

One must not only believe in what one is saying but also that it matters, especially that it matters to the people to whom one is speaking.

Norman Thomas

The secret of being a bore is to tell everything.

Voltaire

To sway an audience, you must watch them as you speak.

C. Kent Wright

studying 🕸

You have to study a great deal to know a little.
Charles de Secondat

Never start on the "next" before you have mastered
the "previous."
Ivan Pavlov

The brighter you are, the more you have to learn.
Don Herold

success 🕸

I was successful because you believed in me.
Ulysses S. Grant
(to Abraham Lincoln)

I can give you a six-word formula for success: Think
things through—then follow through.
Eddie Rickenbacker

Industry is the parent of success.
Anonymous

Success is getting up just one more time than you
fall down.
Anonymous

Success is not a magic ingredient that can be sup-
plied by teachers. Building on strengths allows students to create their own success.
Robert Martin

The common idea that success spoils people by
making them vain, egotistic, and self-complacent is
erroneous; on the contrary, it makes them, for the
most part, humble, tolerant, and kind. Failure makes
people cruel and bitter.
W. Somerset Maugham

There is nothing in the world that will take the chip off of one's shoulder like a feeling of success.
Thomas Wolfe

There is only one success—to be able to spend your life in your own way.
Christopher Morley

To be great we need to win games we aren't supposed to win.
Julius Erving

talent ஐ

Use what talents you possess: the woods would be very silent if no birds sang there except those that sang best.
Henry Van Dyke

Everyone has talent; what is rare is the courage to follow the talent to the dark place where it leads.
Erica Jong

It is a very rare thing for a m an of talent to succeed by his talent.
Joseph Roux

The buried talent is the sunken rock on which most lives strike and founder.
Frederick Faber

There is no such thing as a great talent without great willpower.
Honoré de Balzac

Toil to make yourself remarkable by some talent or other.
Seneca

*Everyone teaches,
everyone learns.*

Arnold Bennett

tardiness ❧

He who is late may gnaw the bones.

Yugoslav proverb

People count up the faults of those who keep them waiting.

French proverb

teachers ❧

It is the supreme art of the teacher to awaken joy in creative expression and knowledge.

Albert Einstein

A good teacher feels his way, looking for response.

Paul Goodman

A good teacher is a determined person.

Gilbert Highet

A teacher affects eternity; he can never tell where his influence stops.

Henry Adams

A teacher who can arouse a feeling for one single good action, for one single good poem, accomplishes more than he who fills our memory with rows on rows of natural objects, classified with name and form.

Goethe

Our chief want in life is somebody who will make us do what we can.

Ralph Waldo Emerson

Everyone who remembers his own educational experience remembers teachers, not methods and techniques. The teacher is the kingpin of the educational situation. He makes and breaks programs.

Sidney Hook

I have learned silence from the talkative, toleration from the intolerant, and kindness from the unkind; yet strange, I am ungrateful to those teachers.
Kahlil Gibran

Kindergarten teacher: One who knows how to make the little things count.
Anonymous

Let such teach others who themselves excel.
Alexander Pope

The students are alive, and the purpose of education is to stimulate and guide their self-development. It follows as a corollary from this premise, that the teachers also should be alive with living thoughts.
Alfred North Whitehead

The true teacher defends his pupils against his own personal influence. He inspires self-trust. He guides their eyes from himself to the spirit that quickens him. He will have no disciple.
Amos Alcott

Unless one has taught...it is hard to imagine the extent of the demands made on a teacher's attention.
Charles Silberman

A teacher is an answer in search of a question.
Anonymous

We teach who we are.
John Gardner

teaching ⚛

In teaching, the greatest sin is to be boring.
J. F. Herbart

Everything I learn about teaching I learn from bad students.
John Holt

Everything should be made as simple as possible, but not one bit simpler.

Albert Einstein

He who receives an idea from me, receives instruction himself without lessening mine; as he who lights his taper at mine, receives light without darkening me.

Thomas Jefferson

If you would thoroughly know anything, teach it to others.

Tryon Edwards

I love to teach as a painter loves to paint, as a musician loves to play, as a singer loves to sing, as a strong man rejoices to run a race. Teaching is an art—an art so great and so difficult to master that a man or a woman can spend a long life at it, without realizing much more than his limitations and mistakes and his distances from the ideal.

William Phelps

If, in instructing a child, you are vexed with it for want of adroitness, try, if you have never tried before, to write with your left hand, and then remember that a child is all left hand.

J. F. Boyse

Men must be taught as if you taught them not,
And things unknown proposed as things forgot.

Alexander Pope

Never tell people how to do things. Tell them *what* to do and they will surprise you with their ingenuity.

George S. Patton

One might as well say he has sold when no one has bought as to say he has taught when no one has learned.

John Dewey

People sometimes say, "I should like to teach if only pupils cared to learn." But then there would be little need of teaching.

George Herbert Palmer

Teaching is not a lost art, but the regard for it is a lost tradition.

Jacques Barzun

Teaching youngsters isn't much like making steel ...and essential as good technique is, I don't think education is basically a technological problem. It is a problem of drawing out of each youngster the best he has to give and of helping him to see the world he is involved in clearly enough to become himself— among other people—in it, while teaching him the skills he will need in the process.

Edgar Friedenberg

The ideal condition would be, I admit, that men should be right by instinct; but since we are all likely to go astray, the reasonable thing is to learn from those who can teach.

Sophocles

The master who has forgotten his boyhood will have poor success.

A. Maclaren

The object of teaching a child is to enable him to get along without his teacher.

Elbert Hubbard

The whole art of teaching is only the art of awakening the natural curiosity of young minds for the purpose of satisfying it afterwards.

Anatole France

To teach is to learn twice.

Joseph Joubert

When you are dealing with a child, keep all your wits about you, and sit on the floor.

Austin O'Malley

126

You could stand all day in a laundry...still in possession of your mind. But this teaching utterly obliterates you. It cuts right into your being: essentially, it takes over your spirit. It drags it out from where it would hide.
Sylvia Ashton-Warner

While we teach, we learn.
Seneca

teenagers ❧

There's nothing wrong with teenagers that reasoning with them won't aggravate.
Anonymous

The main problem with teenagers is that they're just like their parents were at their age.
Anonymous

Why can't life's problems hit us at eighteen, when we know everything?
Anonymous

television ❧

Children who have been taught, or conditioned, to listen passively most of the day to the warm verbal communications coming from the TV screen, to the deep emotional appeal of the so-called TV personality, are often unable to respond to real persons because they arouse so much less feeling then the skilled actor.
Bruno Bettelheim

The Plug-in Drug [title of a book].
Marie Winn

The world could use more vision and less television.
Anonymous

127

There are days when any electrical appliance in the house, including the vacuum cleaner, seems to offer more entertainment possibilities than the TV set.

Harriet Van Horne

textbooks ✿

Many textbooks make the...mistake (of not telling) the reader clearly what he is going to learn. They do not, while he is learning it, show him the relation of each part to the whole. And they usually finish, not with a reasonable conclusion and a glance backwards, but abruptly and even rudely.

Gilbert Highet

thinking ✿

Many of us have been trained not to respect our own thinking, but to feel that we have to depend on the thinking of others. This leads us to acceptance of authority, whether what the authority says makes sense or not.

Earl Kelley

All the problems of the world could be settled easily if men were only willing to think. The trouble is that men very often resort to all sorts of devices in order not to think, because thinking is such hard work.

Thomas Watson

Every man prefers belief to the exercise of judgment.

Seneca

Every man...should periodically be compelled to listen to opinions which are infuriating to him. To hear nothing but what is pleasing to one is to make a pillow of the mind.

John Ervine

Living is a constant process of deciding what we are going to do.

José Ortega y Gasset

Everyone should keep a mental wastepaper basket and the older he grows, the more things he will consign to it.

Samuel Butler

Few minds wear out; more rust out.

Christian Bovee

In training a child to the activity of thought, above all things we must beware of what I will call "inert ideas"—that is to say, ideas that are merely received into the mind without being utilized, or tested, or thrown into fresh combinations.

Alfred North Whitehead

It is well for people who think to change their minds occasionally in order to keep them clean.

Luther Burbank

Most human beings have an almost infinite capacity for taking things for granted.

Aldous Huxley

The only man who can change his mind is a man that's got one.

Edward Noyes Westcott

The shrewd guess, the fertile hypothesis, the courageous leap to a tentative conclusion—these are the most valuable coin of the thinker at work.

Jerome Bruner

There are two ways to slide easily through life: to believe everything or to doubt everything; both ways save us from thinking.

Alfred Korzybski

There is no bore we dread being left alone with so much as our own minds.

James Russell Lowell

Thinking is like living and dying; you must do it for yourself.

Anonymous

130

Thought is great and swift and free, the light of the world, and the chief glory of man.

Bertrand Russell

Thoughts come clearly while one walks.

Thomas Mann

We must learn to welcome and not to fear the voices of dissent. We must dare to think about "unthinkable things" because when things become unthinkable, thinking stops and action becomes mindless.

James Fulbright

When I have nothing to do for an hour, and I don't want to do anything, I neither read nor watch television. I sit back in a chair and let my mind relax. I do what I call idling. It's as if the motorcar's running but you haven't got it in gear. You have to allow a certain amount of time in which you are doing nothing in order to have things occur to you, to let your mind think.

Mortimer Adler

time 𝕰

A day is a miniature Eternity.

Ralph Waldo Emerson

Ordinary people merely think how they shall *spend* their time; a man of talent tries to *use* it.

Arthur Schopenhauer

So teach us to number our days, that we may apply our hearts unto wisdom.

The Bible

Time is like money; the less we have of it to spare, the further we make it go.

Josh Billings

Time is what we want most, but what, alas, we use worst.

William Penn

What would be the use of immortality to a person who cannot use well a half hour?

Ralph Waldo Emerson

troublemakers 🕸

Most of the trouble in the world is caused by people wanting to be important.

T. S. Eliot

The usual excuse of those who cause others trouble is that they wish them well.

Vauvenargues

troubles 🕸

Although the world is very full of suffering, it is also full of overcoming it.

Helen Keller

Don't think there are no crocodiles because the water is calm.

Malayan proverb

Drag your thoughts away from your troubles—by the ears, by the heels, or any other way, so you manage it; it's the healthiest thing a body can do.

Mark Twain

If you want to make someone laugh, tell him your troubles.

Spanish proverb

Is your cucumber bitter? Throw it away. Are there briars in your path? Turn aside. That is enough. Do not go on to say, "Why were things of this sort ever brought into the world?"

Marcus Aurelius

*Life is a series of experiences,
each one of which makes us bigger,
even though sometimes it is hard
to realize this.*

Henry Ford

Learn to see in another's calamity the ills which you should avoid.
Publilius Syrus

The course of true anything never does run smooth.
Samuel Butler

There are people who are always anticipating trouble, and in this way they manage to enjoy many sorrows that never really happen to them.
Josh Billings

There is no education like adversity.
Benjamin Disraeli

Trouble is the common denominator of living. It is the great equalizer.
Ann Landers

Whenever evil befalls us, we ought to ask ourselves, after the first suffering, how we can turn it into good.
Leigh Hunt

trust ೫

The chief lesson I have learned in a long life is that the only way to make a man trustworthy is to trust him; and the surest way to make him untrustworthy is to distrust him and show your distrust.
Henry L. Stimson

You may be deceived if you trust too much, but you will live in torment if you do not trust enough.
Frank Crane

truth ೫

Rather than love, than money, than fame, give me truth.
Henry David Thoreau

As scarce as truth is, the supply has always been in excess of the demand.
Josh Billings

It is and it must in the long run be better for man to see things as they are than to be ignorant of them.
A. E. Houseman

Reason means truth and those who are not governed by it take the chance that someday the sunken fact will rip the bottom out of their boat.
Oliver Wendell Holmes, Jr.

Truth is always exciting. Speak it, then. Life is dull without it.
Pearl Buck

When in doubt, tell the truth.
Mark Twain

underachievers ⚘

Children who are treated as if they are uneducable almost invariably become uneducable.
Kenneth Clark

If they try to rush me, I always say, "I've only got one other speed—and it's slower."
Glenn Ford

Never discourage anyone...who continually makes progress, no matter how slow.
Plato

vacations ⚘

To do great work a man must be very idle as well as very industrious.
Samuel Butler

*A good holiday is one spent
among people whose notions
of time are vaguer than yours.*

J. B. Priestly

A good vacation is over when you begin to yearn for your work.

Morris Fishbein

It is only in adventure that some people succeed in knowing themselves—in finding themselves.

André Gide

My own vision of bliss halfway through a term is solitary confinement in a soundproof cell.

Jacques Barzun

The real problem of your leisure is how to keep other people from using it.

Anonymous

wisdom ॐ

Wisdom consists not so much in knowing what to do in the ultimate as knowing what to do next.

Herbert Hoover

Growth in wisdom may be exactly measured by decrease in bitterness.

Friedrich Nietzsche

He is a fool that cannot conceal his wisdom.

Benjamin Franklin

That which seems the height of absurdity in one generation often becomes the height of wisdom in another.

Adlai Stevenson

The art of being wise is the art of knowing what to overlook.

William James

The door to wisdom swings on hinges of common sense and uncommon thoughts.

Anonymous

Wisdom is knowing what to do next; virtue is doing it.

David Starr Jordan

We can be knowledgeable with other men's knowledge, but we cannot be wise with other men's wisdom.

Montaigne

wonder ॐ

Philosophy begins with wonder.

Socrates

Wonder rather than doubt is the root of knowledge.

Abraham Heschel

Wonder implies the desire to learn.

Aristotle

words ॐ

Words—so innocent and powerless as they are, as standing in a dictionary, how potent for good and evil they become, in the hands of one who knows how to combine them!

Nathaniel Hawthorne

The difference between the right word and the almost right word is the difference between lightning and the lightning bug.

Mark Twain

work & work habits ॐ

Everything considered, work is less boring than amusement.

Charles Baudelaire

Being forced to work, and forced to do your best, will breed in you temperance and self-control, diligence and strength of will, cheerfulness and content, and a hundred virtues which the idle never know.

Charles Kingsley

Be methodical if you would succeed in business or in anything. Whatever your calling, master all its bearings and details, its principles, instruments, and applications. Method is essential if you would get through your work easily and with economy of time.

William Matthews

Don't be afraid to give your best to what seemingly are small jobs. Every time you conquer one it makes you that much stronger. If you do the little jobs well, the big ones will tend to take care of themselves.

Dale Carnegie

Hurry is slow.

Latin proverb

No matter how trifling the matter on hand, do it with a feeling that it demands the best that is in you, and when done look it over with a critical eye, not sparing a strict judgment of yourself.

Sir William Osler

Nothing ever comes to one that is worth having except as a result of hard work.

Booker T. Washington

Nothing is particularly hard if you divide it into small jobs.

Henry Ford

So that in order that a man may be happy, it is necessary that he should not only be capable of his work, but a good judge of his work.

John Ruskin

There is no such thing as a long piece of work, except one that you dare not start.
Charles Baudelaire

When I look back, the greatest thing that ever happened to me is that when I first picked up a basketball, I was terrible. If things come naturally, you may not bother to work at improving them and you can fall short of your potential.
Bob Pettit

When you have a number of disagreeable duties to perform, always do the most disagreeable first.
Josiah Quincy

Work is the only thing. Life may bring disappointments, but work is consolation.
Marcel Proust

writing 🥨

When we see a natural style we are quite amazed and delighted, because we expected to see an author and find a man.
Blaise Pascal

Whatever sentence will bear to be read twice, we may be sure was thought twice.
Henry David Thoreau

Consult a dictionary for proper meanings and pronunciations...I used to thank people for their "fulsome introduction," until I discovered to my dismay that "fulsome" means offensive and insincere.
George Plimpton

English spelling is weird...or is it *wierd?*
Irwin Hill

How many good books suffer neglect through the inefficiency of their beginnings!
Edgar Allan Poe

*For me, the big chore is
always the same—how to begin
a sentence, how to continue it,
how to complete it.*

Claude Simon

I'm very fond of the English language. I tease it, and you tease only the things you love.

Ogden Nash

Learn as much by writing as by reading.

Lord Acton

Never write on a subject without first having read yourself full on it; and never read on a subject till you have thought yourself hungry on it.

Jean Paul Richter

Only the hand that erases can write the true thing.

Meister Eckhart

Put it before them briefly so they will read it, clearly so they will appreciate it, picturesquely so they will remember it and, above all, accurately so they will be guided by its light.

Joseph Pulitzer

Reading maketh a full man, conference a ready man, and writing an exact man.

Francis Bacon

Unless one is a genius, it is best to aim at being intelligible.

Anthony Hope

Vigorous writing is concise. A sentence should contain no unnecessary words, a paragraph no unnecessary sentences, for the same reason that a drawing should have no unnecessary lines and a machine no unnecessary parts. This requires not that the writer make all his sentences short, or that he avoid all detail and treat his subjects only in outline, but that every word tell.

William Strunk

(Writing is) a different name for conversation.

Laurence Sterne

142

For all a rhetorician's rules
Teach nothing but to name his tools.
Samuel Butler

For me, the big chore is always the same—how to
begin a sentence, how to continue it, how to complete it.
*Claude Simon (on winning the 1985
Nobel Prize)*

All the fun's in how you say a thing.
Robert Frost

a final word

To know all things is not permitted.
Horace

author index

Italicized page numbers indicate quotations accompanying illustrations, which may be duplicated elsewhere in the book.

Byron, Lord, 48

Camus, Albert, 109
Carlyle, Thomas, 1, 4, 26, 80, 108
Carnegie, Andrew, 43
Carnegie, Dale, 10, 35, 139
Carpenter, Edmund, 77
Carroll, Lewis, 69
Carter, Hodding, 18, 93
Catherine of Siena, Saint, 95
Cato, 67
Ceram, C. W., 57
Chamfort, Nicolas, 72, 76
Chapman, John, 110
Chartier, Emile, 64
Chekov, Anton, 104, 116
Chesterfield, Lord, 13, 90, 99, 102
Chesterton, G. K., vi, 113
Chilo, 63
Churchill, Winston, 26, 86, 100
Ciardi, John, 104
Cicero, 62
Clare, John, vi, 64
Clark, Kenneth, 135
Clough, Arthur, 118
Cody, Robert, 26
Coleridge, Samuel Taylor, 106, 108
Colton, Charles Caleb, 52
Conant, James Bryant, 26
Condorcet, Marquis de, 23
Confucius, 7, 56, 73, 78
Conrad, Joseph, 67
Considine, Daniel, 45
Coubertin, Baron Pierre de, 23
Cousins, Norman, 108
Crane, Frank, 15, 134
Creighton, Bishop Mandell, 105
Crockett, Davy, 31
Crothers, Samuel, 30, 71, 79

Delaney, Shelagh, 97
Dell, Floyd, 28
Democritus of Abdera, 98
Descartes, René, 35
Dewey, John, 11, 33, 65, 92, 94, 113, 125
Diane, Comtesse, 24
Dickens, Charles, 48
Disney, Walt, 107

Disraeli, Benjamin, 7, 77, 94, 134
Dr. Johnson, v, vii, 4, 28, 53, 60, 71, 73, 74, 84, 88, 95, 114
Dostoevski, Fyodor, 58
Douglas, Norman, 83
Douglass, Frederick, 64
Doyle, Arthur Conan, 78
Dreikurs, Rudolf, 40
Drucker, Peter, 105
Durant, Will and Ariel, vi, 50, 59

Eckhart, Meister, 142
Edison, Thomas A., 10, 75
Edwards, Tryon, 21, 125
Einstein, Albert, 28, 67, 105, 114, 123, 125
Eisenhower, Dwight, 78
Eldridge, Paul, 99
Eliot, T. S., 132
Emerson, Ralph Waldo, vii, 8, 13, 20, 21, 24, 41, 43, 47, 50, 52, 54, 56, 62, 70, 83, 106, 114, 123, 131, 132
Emmons, Nathanial, 64
Epictetus, 57, 58, 119
Erskine, John, 88
Ervine, John, 128
Erving, Julius, 121
Euclid, 84
Evans, Bergen, 35

Faber, Frederick, 88, 121
Fauvel-Gourand, Francis, 84
Feather, William, 31, 41, 81
Fishbein, Morris, 137
Flaubert, Gustav, 62
Flesch, Rudolph, 27
Fonteyn, Margot, 8, 116
Ford, Glenn, 135
Ford, Henry, 10, 47, 52, 69, 133, 139
Fosdick, Harry, 62
France, Anatole, 15, 29, 67, 109, 126
Francis, Brendan, 5, 13, 100
Francis de Sales, Saint, 23, 94
Franklin, Benjamin, 14, 15, 16, 40, 54, 60, 65, 75, 102, 114, 116, 118, 137
Friedenberg, Edgar, 39, 126

Fromm, Erich, 33, 81
Frost, Robert, 36, 143
Fry, Christopher, 97
Fulbright, James, 131
Fuller, Buckminster, 102
Fuller, Margaret, 74
Fuller, Thomas, 56, 77

Galilei, Galileo, 65
Gandhi, Indira, 20
Gandhi, Mohandas, 64, 81
Gardner, John, 44, 111, 124
Gauguin, Paul, 8, 66
Gentry, Dave, 54
George, David Lloyd, 4, 16, 31
Gibbon, Edward, 106
Gibran, Kahlil, 124
Gide, André, 78, 137
Glasgow, Ellen, 10
Glasser, William, 19
Goebner, Nancy, 104
Goethe, 2, 27, 30, 43, 76, 100,
    110, 115, 118, 123
Goodlad, John, 37
Goodman, Paul, 123
Goodwin, Jim, 69
Gourmont, Remy De, 65
Gracián, Baltasar, v, 4, 10, 40
Grande, Marquis De La, 53
Grant, Ulysses S., 120
Grayson, David, 71
Groddeck, Georg, 10
Guinon, Albert, 35, 118

Haecker, Theodore, 48
Half, Robert, 1
Halifax, Lord, 97
Hamerton, Philip, 4
Hamilton, Alexander, 57
Hamilton, Edith, 39
Hardy, G. H., 84
Harris, Sydney, 5, 24, 37, 74
Hart, B. H. Liddell, 53
Haskins, Henry, 69, 77
Hawthorne, Nathaniel, 138
Hayakawa, S. I., 50, 106
Hayes, Helen, 2
Hazlitt, William, 25, 45, 87
Hechinger, Fred, 109
Heine, Heinrich, 13
Hemingway, Ernest, 80
Henri, Robert, 87

Herbart, J. F., 124
Herold, Don, 120
Heschel, Abraham, 138
Highet, Gilbert, 75, 92, 123, 128
Hill, Irwin, 140
Hippocrates, 80
Hitchcock, R. D., 115
Hobbes, John, 25, 55
Hoffer, Eric, 43, 60, 83
Holmes, Oliver Wendell, Jr., 14,
    135
Holt, John, 53, 124
Homer, 2
Hood, Paxton, 11
Hook, Sidney, 123
Hoover, Herbert, 137
Hope, Anthony, 142
Horace, 86, 143
Houseman, A. E., 135
Howard, Sidney, 58
Howe, E. W., 56
Hubbard, Elbert, 8, 25, 28, 31,
    52, 54, 59, 72, 73, 102, 126
Hügel, Baron Friedrich von, 69
Hugo, Victor, 88
Hulbert, Harold, 81
Hume, David, 39
Hunt, Leigh, 134
Huxley, Aldous, 15, 18, 47, 130
Huxley, Thomas, 4, 50, 74, 111

Ibsen, Henrik, 26
Inge, William, 13, 60
Irving, Washington, 58
Iturbi, José, 16

Jackson, Holbrook, 109
Jackson, Jesse, 92
James, Alice, 78
James, William, 10, 21, 40, 57,
    74, 102, 110, 137
Jefferson, Thomas, 4, 19, 20, 36,
    91, 125
Johnson, Samuel. See
    Dr. Johnson
Jones, Franklin, 26
Jong, Erica, 121
Jonson, Ben, 99
Jordan, Barbara, 100
Jordan, David Starr, 138
Joubert, Joseph, 126
Jouvenel, Bertrand de, 71

Pareto, Vilfredo, 86
Parker, Theodore, 102
Partridge, W. S., 92
Pascal, Blaise, 140
Pasternak, Victoria, 50
Pasteur, Louis, 83, 95
Patton, George S., 125
Pavese, Cesare, 59
Pavlov, Ivan, 120
Peguy, Charles, 57
Penn, William, 132
Perls, Fritz, 77
Persius, 3, 94
Peter, Laurence, 5
Petit-Senn, J., 33
Pettit, Bob, 140
Phelps, William, 14, 106, 125
Picasso, Pablo, 7
Pickford, Mary, 52, 85
Plato, 30, 37, 97, 135
Plautus, 94
Plimpton, George, 140
Plomp, John, 16
Plowden Report, 18, 61
Plutarch, 81
Poe, Edgar Allan, 140
Poincaré, Henri, 34
Pollock, Robert, 90
Pope, Alexander, 73, 77, 89, 124, 125
Pound, Ezra, 65
Priestly, J. B., 136
Proust, Marcel, 140
Proverb, 4, 14, 43, 53, 58, 65, 94, 103
  African, 74
  Ashanti, 88
  Chinese, 5, 11, 14, 27, 48, 56, 73
  English, 102
  French, 45, 86, 95, 123
  German, 7, 54, 77
  Hindu, 25
  Italian, 7, 80
  Japanese, 95
  Latin, 72, 139
  Malayan, 132
  Norwegian, 62
  Russian, 83
  Scandinavian, 54
  Scottish, 39
  Spanish, 14, 25, 59, 87, 102, 115, 132

Vermont, 25
Welsh, 81
Yugoslav, vi, 76, 101, 123
Pulitzer, Joseph, 142

Quillen, Robert, 34
Quincy, Josiah, 140
Quintilianus, Marcus Fabius, 87

Raleigh, Sir Walter, 42, 44
Rand, Ayn, 72
Rather, Dan, 40
Reade, Charles, 119
Reading, Lord, 119
Renard, Jules, 13
Repplier, Agnes, 37
Richter, Jean Paul, 15, 142
Rickenbacker, Eddie, 120
Robert, Marc, 30
Rogers, Will, 7, 62, 65
Roosevelt, Eleanor, 41, 74, 78
Roosevelt, Franklin D., vi, 37, 112, 119
Roosevelt, Theodore, 1
Roper, John, 35
Rousseau, Jean Jacques, 92
Roux, Joseph, 121
Rusk, Dean, 81
Ruskin, John, 105, 139
Russell, Bertrand, 18, 35, 58, 67, 84, 131
Rutherford, Mark, 75

Saint-Exupéry, Antoine de, 88
Sandburg, Carl, 27
Santayana, George, ii, 22, 48, 72
Sarnoff, Dorothy, 119
Sarton, May, 19
Sartre, Jean-Paul, 31
Satir, Virginia, 10
Savile, George, 36
Schiller, Johann von, 94
Schopenhauer, Arthur, 65, 131
Schwab, Charles, 40
Schweitzer, Albert, 18, 44, 58
Scully, Frank, vii, 26
Secondat, Charles de, 120
Selden, John, 44
Seneca, i, 65, 111, 116, 121, 127, 128
Shakespeare, William, 45, 71

149

topic index

When a cross-reference pertains to one specific quotation, the author's name is given in parentheses. Otherwise, cross-references are to related topics where you might find a quotation appropriate to your needs.